Team Patterns in Girls' and Women's Basketball

Team Patterns
in Girls' and Women's
Basketball

William E. Warren

South Brunswick and New York: A. S. Barnes and Company
London: Thomas Yoseloff Ltd

A. S. Barnes and Co., Inc.
Cranbury, New Jersey 08512

Thomas Yoseloff Ltd
108 New Bond Street
London W1Y OQX, England

Library of Congress Cataloging in Publication Data

Warren, William E   1941-
    Team patterns in girls' and women's basketball.

    Bibliography: p.
    1. Basketball for women. I. Title.
GV886.W37   796.32'38   74-30979
    ISBN 0-498-01721-4

PRINTED IN THE UNITED STATES OF AMERICA

For Louise, without whom neither this book nor
little else would have been possible; and for
Millie, who could have been the greatest of
them all

Contents

Introduction

The basic purpose of this book is to investigate the unique offensive problems and possibilities of girls' and women's six-player basketball, and thus demonstrate the inaccuracy of the long held belief that, from a coaching standpoint, women's basketball is merely a form of the men's game. Men and women coaches alike, have generally failed to acknowledge the existence within girls' basketball of a legitimate body of knowledge with its own particular problems, techniques, and strategies.

Investigation of the literature reveals an enormous output advantage in favor of boys' basketball, but it also shows an unexpected lack of analytical range and depth within the literature of girls' and women's basketball. While hundreds of books have been written on various aspects of boys' basketball, an in-depth study of the unique aspects of girls' basketball has been virtually nonexistent as far as the literature is concerned. Practically all of the coaching books concerning girls' basketball have been either generalized overviews of the sport or brief summaries occurring within books dealing with team sports for girls or women. Thus far, very little of the creative potential in girls' basketball has been tapped.

For example, one of the most difficult problems confronting a coach in any team sport is that of beating the presses, especially the half-court presses in girls' basketball. There is nothing in the boys' literature that can shed light upon the situation, but there is little more information available on the subject in the girls' literature.

Consider for a moment the subject of bibliographies. How often have books for girls' coaches been cited as sources for basketball methods or information in boys' basketball? How often has the converse been true? Admittedly, the boys have been "firstest with the mostest," but the two week interval between the first boys' and girls' games in 1891 should have been caught up with by now. Why it has not is perhaps indicative of many things, one being the fact that we have been slow to recognize the potential of girls' basketball for unique contributions to the art and science of basketball.

This is not to say that everything contained within the pages of this book is unique, indeed, much of it is borrowed or adapted from boys' basketball. That should not, however, diminish its potential for original contribution to the literature.

Nor does the author wish to impute a sense of finality or completeness to any or all of the material covered in this book. It should be considered a beginning—no more, and certainly no less, a step in the direction of parity between the two branches of basketball as far as the literature is concerned. Coaching girls' basketball is not easier than coaching boys' basketball because the girls play a slower game, just as coaching boys is not easier than coaching girls because of the predominance of literature in their favor. Both are difficult to do properly, but the task of coaching girls' and women's basketball will be greatly facilitated when its professional literature achieves a scope and range comparable to the boys' literature.

Explanation Of Diagrams

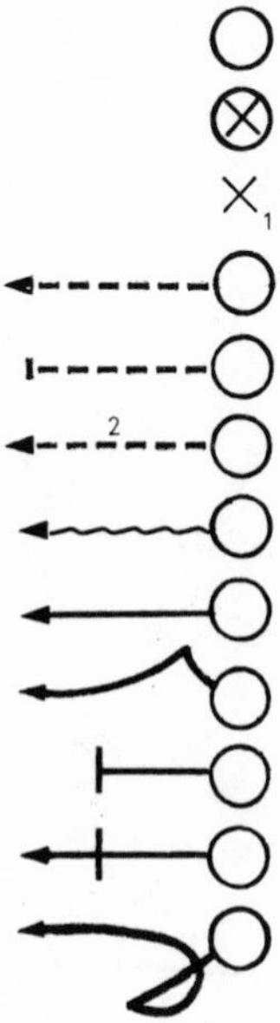

○   Offensive Player (Forward)

⊗   Offensive Player With Ball

$\times_1$ Defensive Player #1 (Guard)

◄------○   Pass

I------○   Fake Pass

◄--²--○   Second Pass In A Series

◄∼∼∼∼○   Path Of Dribbler

◄------○   Offensive Movement Without Ball

◄⌐⌐○   Fake In One Direction, Cut In Another

├──○   Screen

◄─┼─○   Pick

◄∽○   Reverse Pivot

Team Patterns
in Girls' and Women's
Basketball

Part I
TEAM OFFENSE

Shoot, if you must . . .

J. G. Whittier
Barbara Frietchie

1
Zone Offenses

WHAT IS A ZONE?

Basically, a zone defense sets the defensive players' responsibilities in terms of particular areas on the court and, although they move around and shift defensive assignments constantly, they remain in or near their zone and guard players only when they enter that particular zone.

Almost all coaches use zone defenses occasionally. Some coaches use them sparingly if at all, while other coaches place a tremendous amount of confidence in the variety of the zone defenses available. In the end, however, each coach will use whatever defense is likely to create the most problems for the offense.

Zone defenses are used to attack the opponent's offensive weakness or hide some kind of defensive weakness. Zones can be used to protect players in foul trouble; to increase the chances of keeping the ball outside when a team would prefer to work inside; to shut off passing lanes; to keep defensive players in position to fast break effectively when the ball changes hands; to increase rebounding strength; to reduce fouls; to discourage a team from taking high-percentage shots, especially when that team has only one or two offensive scoring threats; and to simplify the defensive movements of a fundamentally weak defensive team.

The coach who chooses to deploy a zone defense should do so with the knowledge that all zone defenses have inherent weaknesses which the offense may exploit. First, zones do not lend themselves easily to overloading without creating unfavorable matchups. Second, they permit the offense to attack the zones' vulnerable areas, or to match up stronger offensive threats against weaker defenders. Finally, the defensive players (guards) have a more narrow range of movement in zone defenses than in player-to-player defenses. As a result they are sometimes lulled into rhythmic adjustments to the constant movement of the ball, thereby allowing a passiveness to seep into their pattern of defense.

The basic zone defenses employed in girls' and women's basketball are: 2–2; 1–2–1; 1–3; 2–1–1; 1–1–2; and combination zones such as the Triangle-One and various matchup zones, that combine zone and player-to-player principles and may appear as any of the above.

ZONE SITUATIONS

Basic Outside Patterns.

The most elementary zone patterns are those in which the offensive players (forwards) line up outside and either shift to one side in some type of overload (Diagrams 1 & 2), or stay in their basic positions, the most familiar being shown in Diagrams 3 and 4.

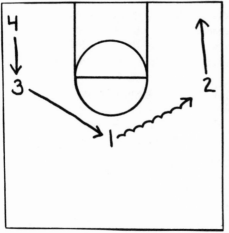

Diag. 1   Outside Overload

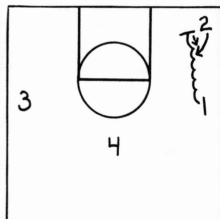

Diag. 2   Simple Screen Off Basic Overload

The object of outside patterns may be seen again in Diagrams 3/4 where the defenses are in 2–2 and 1–2–1 zones. Such patterns, designed to split the defense by aligning the players in that zone's weakest points, are effective when the defense is extremely slow to react, or reluctant to leave the basket or free throw lane. The weakness of these outside patterns is that, when they are not involved beyond their basic structure, no further defensive movement is necessary once the guards react to the primary offensive movements.

Diag. 3   Splitting The 2–2 Zone Outside

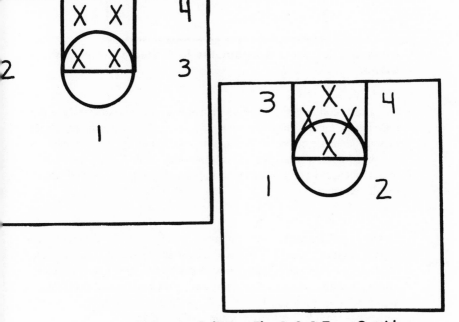

Diag. 4   Splitting The 1–2–1 Zone Outside

For example, in the single-cutter-through pattern shown in Diagram 5, only one defensive adjustment is necessary, no matter how many times the pattern is repeated.

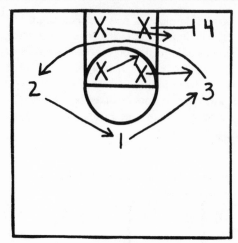

Diag. 5   Defensive Adjustments To A Single Cutter, Ball In Corner

Whether confronted with aggressive pressure defense or sinking zones that clog the middle, the team that passively tosses the ball around outside or sends a single cutter through the middle hoping for a return pass, is grasping for straws that do not exist. They may succeed against mediocre teams, but against good teams their shot charts will be as unblemished as the driven snow.

Inside Cutters

Although there are an infinite number of ways to send a player through a zone in order to create movement and/or confusion on the part of the defense, two examples should suffice for demonstration purposes. First, sending a wing through to the opposite corner from a 1–2–1 offensive alignment (Diagram 6), and second, sending a cutter through after a corner pass in a 2–2 offensive setup. (Diagram 7)

In the first instance, an overload is created, thereby putting pressure on the outmanned defenders on that side of the court. In the second case, not only the pass to the corner, but also the cutter's movement and resultant rotation of the other offensive players, will force the defense out of its basic position.

Diag. 6 Basic Offensive Overload

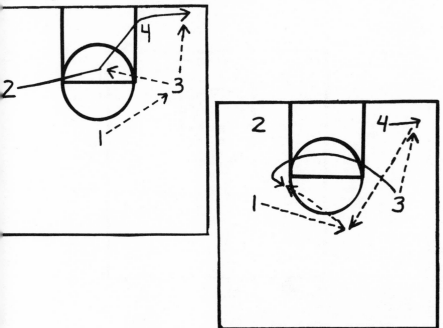

Diag. 7 Single Cutter Through, Return Pass

The weakness of these patterns—if it is indeed a weakness, for they may prove to be ideal ways to attack a team's particular weak points—is that, once the defense adjusts to the cutters' movements, no further major defensive movements are necessary.

While the outside cutters generally work for corner or other perimeter shots, plays involving inside cutters begin with the attempt to get the open inside shot, especially the six to eight foot shot inside the free throw lane.

Attacking the 2–2 Zone Defense

Possibly the easiest way to attack a 2–2 zone, although not necessarily the most effective, is to split the defense as was shown in Diagram 3, or modify it slightly as is shown in Diagrams 8–10.

Diag. 8–10 Splitting Patterns

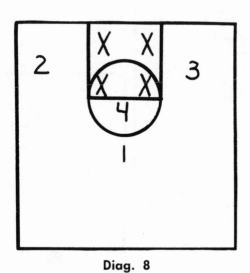

Diag. 8

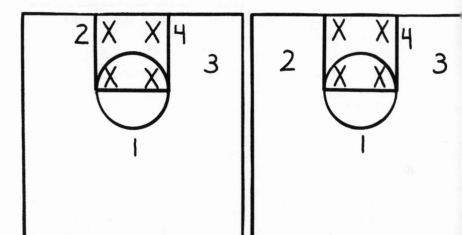

Diag. 9   Diag. 10

In the first case, the corner forward has been moved to a low post position, and in the second, a wing has been dropped low to form a double low post. The low post is important because it tends to keep the defense from guarding the wings too closely.

The positioning of wings O2 and O3 is optional, and usually is governed by the defensive players who guard them. If the inside guards come out on them, the wings line up *higher* (i.e., farther out from the baseline) and, conversely, if the outside guards cover them, the offense may choose to either (a) set the wings *lower,* or nearer the baseline, (b) have the point forward dribble through the outside guards to the free throw line, or (c) move the low post to a high post position, as in Diagram 8.

Actually, the first movement in any of the three alignments is O1's attempt to penetrate the outside guards. If she can force at least one of them to guard her, they will be unable to sag off to guard the wings, and the wing on either side of the court will have an open twelve to fifteen foot shot. The movement of O1 toward the center of the free throw lane freezes the defense in all cases except those when the defense is deploying some kind of matchup zone. The alignment in Diagram 9 does not lend itself to such an attacking movement except in certain cases that will be described later in this section.

A basic setup, such as the one in Diagram 10, can be adequate, especially when a team has only one large girl. Many teams use no more than the basic pattern consisting of penetrating, passing to the forward on the low post's side, and, when the inside guard comes out to guard the wing, passing inside to the low post.

When the outside guards line up wide to defense the passes to the wings, simply by moving the low post to a high post position can be effective as shown in Diagram 8, O1 passes directly to O4, who immediately pivots toward the basket. At the same time the wings go to the basket, forcing a three–on–two situation upon the defense.

Another way of achieving the same situation is shown in Diagram 11. This time, however, as the pass goes to either wing, O4 rolls into the lane and receives the pass from the wing for an open shot, or pass to the opposite wing breaking to the basket. In the play system immediately following, this offensive formation is called "Four-High," because O4 sets up on the high post. In the same way, Diagram 10 is "Two-High".

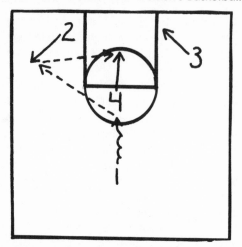

Diag. 11   Hitting The High Post ("Four-High")

After introducing the idea of penetrating the middle as an adjunct to basic offensive formations against the 2–2 zone, an entire system of plays involving cutters can be formulated. In such a system, the called plays would refer to both the cutters involved, and to the players' basic positions.

The basic formation in this series is shown in Diagram 9. With the exception of "Two-High" (see Diagram 10), where O2 sets up at a wing position, O2 always sets up at the low post opposite O4.

The first option is designated "One," because the point forward, O1, is the cutter. After the pass to the wing, O1 continues into the lane to receive the return pass. If O1 is covered and unable to receive the return pass, she continues on to assume O2's low post position. O3 moves to the top of the circle, or (not shown in Diagram 12) to the corner of the free throw lane where she should be momentarily clear. O4 then moves out to O3's wing position.

In option "Two," as O1 dribbles diagonally to her left O2 breaks into the lane, thereby freezing the outside guard on that side. (Diagram 13.)

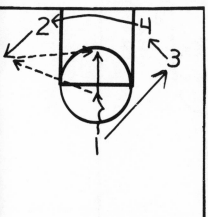

Diag. 12 Option "One"

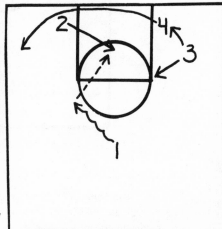

Diag. 13 Option "Two"

O4 cuts across the lane behind the inside guards and continues outside slightly. O3 moves either to the corner of the free throw line to freeze the other outside guard, or toward the basket. If O2 does not receive the inside pass, she continues across the lane to fill either the position of O3 or O4.

These movements designed to facilitate the inside pass to O2 have, in effect, rotated the offense into a "Two-High" setup, with each of the inside forwards (O2, O3, and O4) occupying a new position.

There are two ways to set up shots off option "Three". (Diagram 14) The first method involves O1 who attacks the defense diagonally toward O3's side as O3 breaks into the lane, using a bounce pass to get the ball past the outside guard. If the outside guard sinks off O1, she should fake

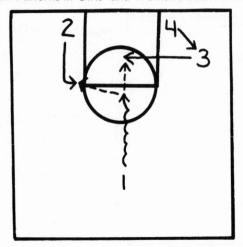

Diag. 14   Option "Three"

the pass inside and take the shot. A greater problem is the possibility that the outside guard will *not* sink off O1, leaving O3 to be guarded by the inside guard on that side. In such cases, O4 will be open for a lob pass under the basket.

A second way of setting up option "Three" is for O1 to penetrate between the outside guards, as O3 breaks into the lane and O2 moves out to the corner of the free throw lane. If O3 cannot get the ball, O1 and O2 will have a two-on-one situation with the outside guard. O4 breaks outside, and O3 moves into the vacated low post position. The same pattern can then be repeated, with O4 cutting into the lane and O3 breaking outside.

Option "Four-Low," Diagram 15, involves O4 cutting into the lane as O1 penetrates, with O3 moving toward the basket. (Note that O3 should not go all the way to the basket except when the pass is made to O4.) If O4 does not receive the pass, she continues on to the high post, where she is in position for "Four-High".

These options are not designed to "carry" a team against 2–2 zones.

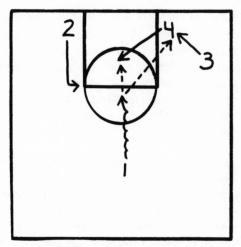

Diag. 15   Option "Four-Low"

They are as ineffective without outside shooting as the outside patterns are without inside penetration. The inside options can be effectively blocked out, but not without giving up the outside shot.

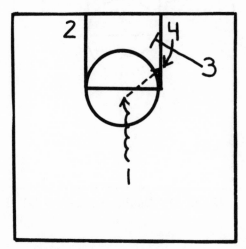

Diag. 16   Option "34-Low"

Option "34 Low," Diagram 16, does not involve the inside cut by O3, but it is a logical movement when the defense is keyed for the inside cut. As O1 penetrates, O3 screens the inside guard on the side of O4, and O4 moves out to receive the pass from O1. She should then be open for a six to ten-foot shot. Other options involving screens (e.g., "21", "31", "42", etc.), are similar extensions of this system.

Several other methods exist for attacking 2–2 zones. For instance, the alignment in Diagram 16 can be altered slightly to produce an excellent double screen for O1. O3 moves to the baseline. (It might be noted that all O4 has to do is set a screen and O3 will be clear for a baseline shot at this point.) O4 crosses the lane behind O2 and receives the pass if open. If not, she sets a screen on the outside guard on that side. O2 screens out the inside guard, and when O1 dribbles to that side, she has a clear shot, or a screen-and-roll situation with O2 or O4. (Diagram 17)

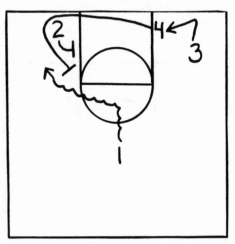

Diag. 17   Double Screen For O1

A zone offense that has had a moderate degree of success is the "Flip-Flop," especially efficient in clearing the corner shooter for an unmolested shot. All four offensive players line up on one side of the court. O1 plays between the top of the circle and the sideline, O2 lines up on the baseline out from the basket, O4 is at the low post, and O3 sets up at high post. (Diagram 18)

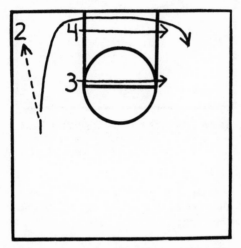

Diag. 18 The Flip-Flop, 1st Half

When the pass is made to O2 in the corner, both O4 and O3 simultaneously flip-flop to the other side of the free throw lane, a move intended to draw the guards on that side out of position. O1 curls to the basket, receiving the pass for a layup if the guards are not aware of the switch. If she does not get the pass, O1 circles back to her original position. The high and low posts then flip-flop back to their original positions and O2 can shoot whenever she is clear. (Diagram 19)

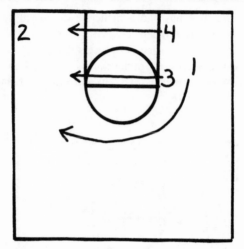

Diag. 19   The Flip-Flop, 2nd Half

For further analysis of attacking 2–2 zone defenses, the reader is referred to the following sections on forcing one-on-one situations and combatting matchup zones.

Attacking The 1–2–1 Zone Defense.

The 1–2–1, or ''Diamond'' zone defense, is among the most versatile of all defenses in girls' basketball. Its basic setup has three girls in rebounding position instead of two, one of whom will *always* be in good rebounding position, a necessity for teams with only one outstanding rebounder. Its outside guard tends to discourage offensive penetration off the dribble, and it lends itself wonderfully to matchup situations such as a combination defense.

The easiest ways to attack a 1–2–1 zone are to split the defense outside as was shown in Diagram 4, or to match up in one-on-one situations. However, although the former will work when the defensive rebounding is so weak that the outside guard has the responsibility of guarding both outside forwards, it will not work against a 1–2–1 matchup zone. The latter will work when the matchup favors the offense, such as when the offense has an outstanding forward, but it, too, will fail when the forwards are not fundamentally sound enough to operate one-on-one.

Rather than conceding defensive superiority to the opponents, a coach must assume that their defense has weaknesses that can be discovered by probing, else they would be in a player-to-player defense. After all, if the guards' rebounding and defensive skills were effective in all situations, the opponents would have no need for any type of zone defense.

Attacking the middle of the 1–2–1 for six to eight foot shots is difficult, except when the forwards are clearly superior to the guards. This is because defensive coverage requires so little margin for error, and also, because the deep guard covers *all* inside cutters until they leave the middle.

The most vulnerable areas of the 1–2–1 are at the corners of the free throw lane, and they can be attacked effectively from a "13" alignment as shown in Diagram 20. O2 and O3 should be lined up even with, and approximately two steps from, the corners of the free throw line. O4 is centered at the high post, and O1 stays comfortably outside until initiating this particular play.

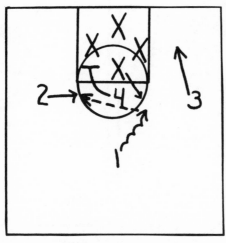

Diag. 20 "13"

The first movement in ''13'' involves O4 setting a screen on the guard at whichever side of the lane she chooses. Her screen should not be set between the guard and the wing receiving the pass, but *between the guard and the point where the wing forward will receive the pass.* Simultaneous with O4's movement to one side of the lane, O1 dribbles diagonally forward toward the opposite corner of the lane, in order to draw the outside guard away from the ball and eliminate the possibility of the wing's being double-teamed. The wing toward which O1 dribbles, clears to the opening on her side of the court.

If the outside guard fails to cover O1, she will be clear for the foul line shot, or she can pass to O3 if the guard on that side covers O1.

The most natural defensive adjustment to ''13'' brings the deep guard out to the high post, while the outside guard moves in front of O4. In this case, an alert O4 will have a layup if the defense switches. (Diagram 21)

A variation that can produce a layup if the defense is not alert in the above situation, is for O4 to clear *outside* the lane after screening. O2 receives the pass from O1, and immediately looks for O3 breaking in front of the guard on her side. (Diagram 22)

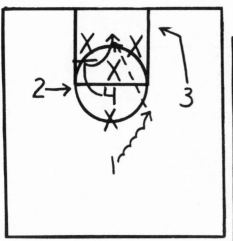

Diag. 21 "13" With Inside Roll

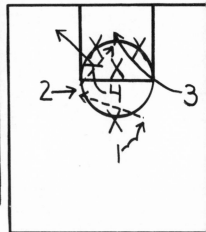

Diag. 22 "13" With O3 Cutti

Incidentally, the system of set plays involving cutters through the middle will also work against a 1–2–1 zone defense when the basic alignment is modified to resemble that shown in Diagram 4. Although the 2–2 setup is not as effective in splitting the 1–2–1 zone defense as the 1–2–1 series attacking the 2–2 zone (the ballhandler often has difficulty in forcing the guards to double-team her, and the size and angle of the passing lanes is diminished in the 2–2 alignment), it can be extremely effective when the dribbler can force the double-team.

Plays and players are numbered as previously described, but the responsibility for attacking the seam between the outside and wing guard is divided between the two outside forwards: O1 attempts to force the double-team in plays "2" and "3" (Diagrams 24, 25), and O3 penetrates in "1" and "4". (Diagrams 23, 26)

Diag. 23 Cutting Pattern "One" Against 1–2–1 Zone

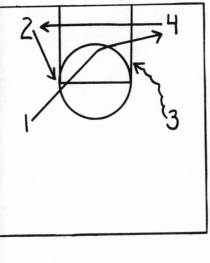

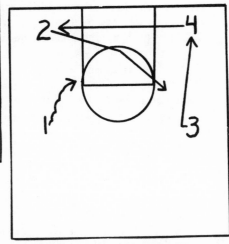

Diag. 24 "2" With Rotation

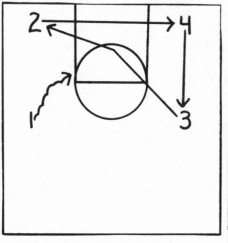

Diag. 25 "3" With Rotation

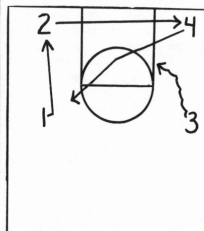

Diag. 26 "4" With Rotation

Movement begins as the dribbler advances between the point and wing guards, followed by the designated cutter breaking into and diagonally across the lane. This precedes the filling of the vacated positions by the other forwards. They rotate in a clockwise direction in ''3'' and ''4'', counterclockwise in ''1'' and ''2''. The dribbler must be able to penetrate deep enough to draw the double-team, then either pass inside, shoot, or find open teammates.

The timing of the forwards' movements is all-important to the success of the inside break and outside cuts. The dribbler must pass inside at the exact moment when the cutter is open, and when the cutter is not open she should not have to wait for other cutters to reach their positions. If the inside cutter breaks too soon, she will be across the lane and out before the ballhandler is ready to pass inside, and the defense will have no difficulty in matching up. Similarly, if the outside cutters take too long in getting to their positions, the dribbler will have no one to pass to if she stops dribbling or is double-teamed.

The easiest way to key the movement of the forwards is to chronologize them, or set them in order. For example, in play number ''4'', the first movement after O3 begins dribbling toward the defensive seam is for 2 to cut across the lane. This movement, designed to help freeze the wing guard and/or provide a passing outlet when the defense stops the inside pass, should occur before O4's break into and across the lane.

The formation described above may be used to combat a 1–2–1 match-up zone by having the forwards remain in their new positions rather than return to their original positions if the inside pass is not achieved. The constant pressure of the attacking dribble from position O1 or O3, combined with inside cutters and outside rotation, affords the guards little opportunity to realign their defense to avoid new and unfavorable matchups.

When the ballhandler fails in her attempt to pass inside, she may retreat slightly until the other forwards reach their new positions. She then may pass and cut into the lane herself to form a continuity pattern, as the other forwards move to fill the vacated positions. Although zone continuity offenses, such as the preceding and those that will be shown in Diagrams 35/39, are not as prevalent as player-to-player continuity patterns, there is no reason why they will not work, as long as the threat of the inside pass keeps the defense honest.

The set play shown in Diagram 27 provides a fine ten to twelve foot

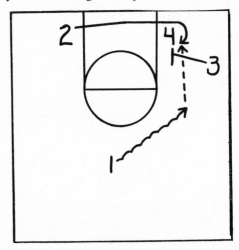

Diag. 27   Double Screen Against 1–2–1 Zone Defense

baseline shot against a 1–2–1 zone defense. O1 dribbles to her right as O3 moves low to set a double screen with O4. O2 cuts across the lane and behind the double screen to receive the pass and attempt to shoot.

A variation in the screening pattern (Diagram 28) can provide an even closer shot for O2, providing that the forwards can synchronize their movements properly. As O1 begins dribbling right, O3 moves low and into the lane, setting a pick on the inside guard and continuing out of the lane. O2 begins her cut simultaneous with the move of O1. After waiting for O3 to pass her, O4 screens the wing guard on her side, then moves quickly out of the lane and to the corner of the free throw line or beyond. If their timing is correct, O2 will be free momentarily for a four to eight foot shot at the baseline.

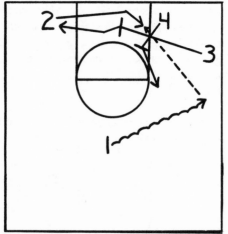

Diag. 28   Variation Of Double-Screening Pattern

Attacking the 1–1–2, 2–1–1, and 1–3 Zone Defenses

These defenses are usually deployed to disguise or negate either a vital rebounding, or defensive, problem that a 2–2 or 1–2–1 zone cannot overcome. For example, Team A might have two tall forwards who play the offensive low post position on either side of the lane, and Team B's inside guards, although adequate, simply cannot contain them one-on-

one. By dropping back one wing guard from a 1–2–1 zone to help out inside, thus shifting from a 1–2–1 zone to a 1–3 setup, the chances of stopping the inside forwards from scoring is increased, although the possibility of the outside forwards' scoring is increased also.

Although their purpose is to provide the greatest defensive strength where the offense is strongest, the 1–1–2, 1–3, and 2–1–1 zone defenses are extremely vulnerable to attack, especially by outside splitting patterns. As such, most coaches use them only sparingly. They usually require little offensive movement to provide the forwards with good shots and, despite their best intentions, they often allow the forwards to match up in unequal one-on-one situations. Diagrams 29–33 show the various attacks.

Diag. 29 Attacking The 1–3 Zone

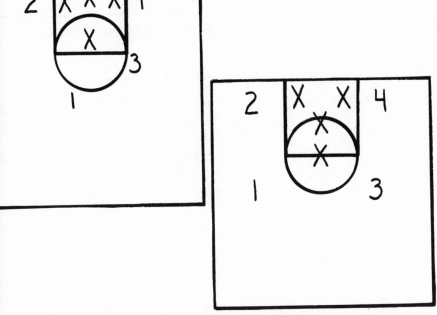

Diag. 30 Attacking The 1–1–2 Zone

Diag. 31   Attacking The 1–1–2 Zone

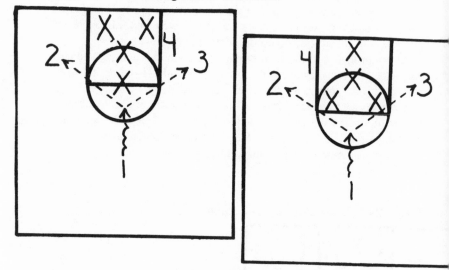

Diag. 32   Attacking The 2–1–1 Zone

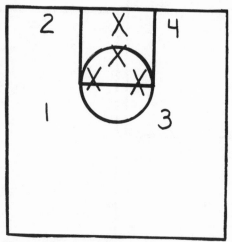

Diag. 33   Attacking The 2–1–1 Zone

Forcing One-On-One Situations

Not all zone offenses attempt to split the defense outside, overload one side of the court with forwards, or send cutters through the middle of the zone. Sometimes a team's best offensive strategy is merely to match up with the defense. For example, when the defense is in a 2–2 zone, the offense also sets up 2–2, or similarly, in a 1–2–1 alignment if the defense is in a Diamond zone.

Why should a coach want to match up offensively? This enables his team to attack outside guards who are weaker fundamentally than the inside guards (or vice versa); to avoid double-teaming of the better forwards: to put pressure on guards in foul trouble; or to simplify offensive maneuvers and cut down ballhandling mistakes by a team whose scoring attack is unbalanced.

For example, a team whose leading scorer is also the best ballhandler and rebounder might set her at low post against zone defenses, passing the ball in to her for short hooks or turnaround jump shots. The simple strategy is to get the ball to her and keep out of her way. The defense can usually be kept from double-teaming her by matching up with them.

An old pattern that often yields an open foul line jump shot is crisscrossing the forwards, with the dribbler passing and screening for the other outside forward. This can be accomplished against weak outside guards in a matchup situation even if the maneuver fails to yield a clear shot, for the outside guards will be unable to drop back to double-team the forwards at the low posts. (Diagram 34)

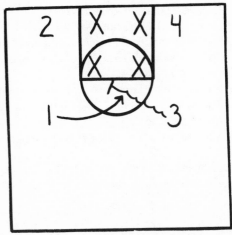

Diag. 34   Outside Crisscross From Matchup

Overloads provide an excellent way of forcing zone defenses into one-on-one coverage. Using the previous example of a team with one tall forward, an overload such as the one described below will either permit her to go one-on-one from two to six feet out, or free another forward for a fifteen foot baseline shot if the low post is double-teamed.

Overloads with all four forwards on one side of the court almost inevitably fail because (a) they allow too many people (eight) in an area too small to accommodate them; (b) the time required to rotate across the court is too great; and (c) they nullify the threat of passing back across the zone. The purpose of overloads is to spread out the defense while retaining positions close enough to the basket to make outside shots feasible. They are not designed to put as many people as possible on one side of the court. Therefore, an overload pattern should have exactly three forwards on one side of the court for best results.

The basic overload alignment has O3 or O4 along the baseline, fifteen to eighteen feet out from the basket, with the other at the low post. O1 begins her move approximately midway between the sideline and the free throw line. O2 may be placed at the free throw line, at the low post away from the ball, or farther out on the side of the court opposite the ball. At the low post opposite O3/O4, O2 is in excellent rebounding position on overshots, and she can also manage a layup if the defense fails to react quickly when the ball is passed inside to O3 or O4. For rotation purposes, O2 serves best at the high post, moving to the basket only when shots are taken.

This offense is built around the baseline shot and the pass inside to the low post. It is effective against *all* zone defenses.

The first movement is O1 dribbling toward the low post. (O4 in Diagram 35, O3 in Diagram 36) She continues until challenged, then passes to the low post or corner. If unchallenged, O1 should shoot rather than pass the ball to a teammate.

If O3 receives the pass in the corner, she *must* take the open shot until the defense challenges her, otherwise, they will merely drop back to double-team the low post. The options of O3 are to (a) shoot from the baseline; (b) pass inside to O4 when the defense comes out; or (c) pass back to O1.

The ball should be passed to the low post whenever the opportunity arises. She is never more than six feet away from the basket, ideal for

Diag. 35 Overload With Defense

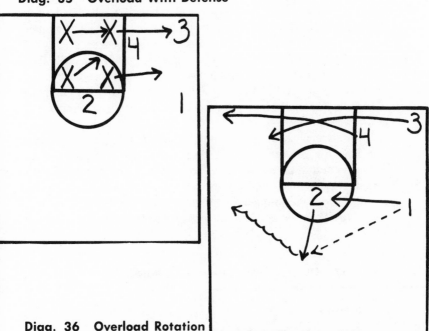

Diag. 36 Overload Rotation

turnaround jump shots, drives, or hook shots. If she is alert, she can sometimes pass across the lane to O2 when she is at the low post opposite the ball.

After passing to the corner or low post, O1 waits for a return pass, then breaks away from the basket to receive it. At the same time, O2 breaks toward midcourt to receive O1's pass, then dribbles to the other side of the court to begin the rotation. O3 and O4 exchange positions on the other side of the court.

Any of several methods of rotation can be used to suit a team's particular needs. Variations for special situations might include:

a. A team with a good corner shooter and/or a good low post player, will retain their positions on both sides of the court;

b. A team with two tall forwards might set them both at low post, with O2 in the corner, rotating only O1 and O2; or

c. A small team, or a team with no experienced post players, might strive for rapid rotation from side to side, hoping to shoot before the defense is ready. The idea here is to lull them into mechanical rotation, then pass quickly back across the zone to open shooters.

A revolving rotation suitable to the requirements of Example C above is easily constructed. O1 passes to O4 in the corner, then clears to the other side of the court. As O4 receives the pass, low post O2 moves outside for a possible return pass, and O3 crosses the lane to become the new low post.

If O4 does not shoot, or cannot pass inside to O3, she passes to O2, who either tries to work the ball inside or back to the corner, or passes the ball crosscourt to O1 as quickly as possible. O3 moves to the opposite corner, O4 goes to the opposite low post, and O2 returns to her low post position. The team has rotated to the other side of the court, and when O1 passes to O3 in the corner, the pattern will begin again. (Diagrams 37–39)

Diag. 37   Overload With Revolving Rotation

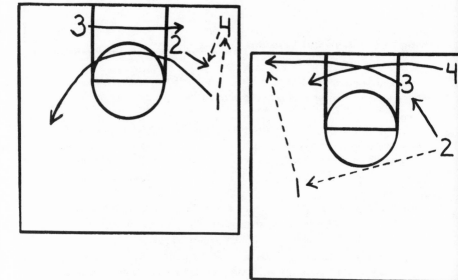

Diag. 38   Revolving Rotation Continued

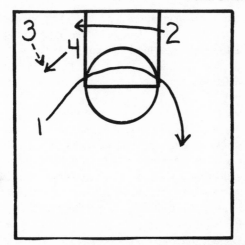

Diag. 39   Revolving Rotation Completed

Sometimes it is easier to dribble outside than to pass to the low post breaking outside, (as in Diagram 38) especially when she is overguarded. In such situations, the corner forward should automatically dribble outside while the low post breaks to the corner position and the offside forward moves across the lane as she normally does whenever the low post vacates her position. (Diagram 40)

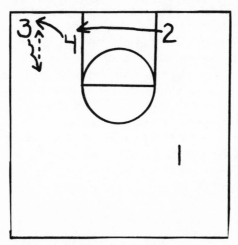

Diag. 40   Alternate Method Of Taking Ball Outside In Revolving Rotation

All they did was switch positions, and the pattern is ready to be rotated to the other side of the court if no shooting opportunities are readily available. The low post breaking to the corner will almost invariably be open though, since the inside guard will be the victim of a blind two-on-one situation.

Overloads such as the one described may also be used as delay or slowdown tactics, although the outside forwards must be particularly careful to break away from their guards to receive passes.

Finally, overloads that rotate not only from one side of the court to the other, but also rotate the players occupying each position, can wreak havoc upon an opponent's attempts to match up within a zone defense.

Combatting The Special Defenses

The two reasons for describing any defensive alignment or strategy as "special" are that they are seen only rarely, or that they require specialized defensive skills, knowledge, and attitudes. Of the two, the latter is a more potent reason for respecting teams employing special defenses. In each of the special defenses (the matchup zone, the combination zone, and the trapping zone) success depends upon aggressive execution to a greater extent than do the regular zone defenses.

For example, when a team is trapping the ball in the corner, they had better be successful, because the offense has a three-on-two advantage every time they *do not* contain the ball in the corner. Similarly, the team using a matchup zone that does not stop inside passes to high-scoring forwards is definitely in the wrong defense.

Special defenses require special skills, but more importantly they require an aggressive attitude in order to avoid giving the offense an advantage. They are based on calculated risks, weighing their disadvantages against the belief that increasing the pressure on some or all of the forwards will swing the advantage toward the defense. The greatest difficulty posed by special defenses is that they are designed to be *attacking* defenses, and attacking an aggressive defense is always a difficult proposition.

MATCHING ZONE DEFENSES

Of all the zone defenses, the most difficult to attack is a matchup zone. Although the guards will not always set up 1–2–1 against a 1–2–1 offense, they will match up defensive responsibilities as if they were in a 1–2–1, and the offense will be unable to find the open shot by splitting the zone outside. The team that matches up is likely to be a fine defensive team, since the matchup zone is also the most difficult zone to operate in terms of concentration, alertness, and reaction.

Briefly, a matchup zone works as follows. When Team A comes downcourt and sets up in a 2–2 zone defense, Team B is likely to set up outside in a 1–2–1 alignment, splitting the defense as was shown in Diagrams 3 and 8. If Team A assumes player-to-player responsibilities within their zone, Team B will be forced to make adjustments of their offensive alignment or strategy. (Diagram 41)

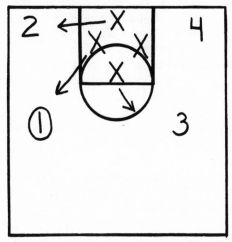

Diag. 41   Matching Up In A 1–2–1 Zone Defense

Note that after the defense shifts toward their player-to-player assignments, they appear to be in either a 2–2 zone, or a player-to-player defense. They are not. Although they may adjust into any of several defensive alignments when the offense sets up, and they may have player-to-player responsibilities within their zone, they are still playing a 1–2–1 zone defense. The 1–2–1 alignment is used as a matchup defense more often than any other kind of zone defense, due to the difficulty in splitting or overloading against a 1–2–1. The only effective splitting alignment is the 2–2, and the ease with which the Diamond shifts into 2–2 coverage has been explained. Also, the 1–2–1 adapts well to overloading because three guards are within one step of either side of the court in their basic positions.

An excellent way to foil the matchups, at least temporarily, is to move the personnel into more favorable matchups. For example, if a team's principal scoring threats are an adequate ballhandler and an outstanding corner shooter, they might be used effectively in an offense similar to the one shown in Diagram 5. The ballhandler passes to the corner and breaks toward the basket, giving them two opportunities to score, either the corner shot, or the pass inside to the cutter.

Unfortunately, the opponents know that the corner shooter is a poor ballhandler, so they can overplay the cutter, thereby shutting off the inside pass. They can then send a tall girl outside to harass the corner forward, aware that she will not drive.

The offense can combat these matchups by moving their shooter to the offside high post, by setting another forward in the corner, and by rotating the ball from the baseline around to the shooter at the corner of the free throw lane. They are using the same offense, but by adjusting their personnel and the spot from where the shot is to be taken, they increase their chances of defeating the matchups.

The greatest obstacle to success in using matchup zones is movement by the offense, especially the inside cutters who alter the offensive thrust. The more cutters presented to the defense, the greater the possibility of defensive mistakes. For instance, it is difficult enough to play a 1–2–1 zone defense from a 2–2 alignment, but when cutters constantly change the shape of the offensive attack, the guards can easily become confused about their defensive responsibilities.

Overloads will sometimes work against matchups, especially when the offense has one or more forwards who work well inside. The act of forcing one-on-one situations is nothing more than matching up offensively.

Overload, shift players around, use cutters to confuse the matchups, anything that keeps pressure on the defense will lessen the effect of matchup defenses.

TRAPPING ZONE DEFENSES

Actually, the terms *trapping* and *matching up* are misleading. A team does not set up in a trapping or matchup zone, it sets up in a certain zone defense and uses trapping or matching up as a means of putting defensive pressure on the forwards.

Trapping is a defensive maneuver in which the guards attempt to double-team the ballhandler in order to steal the ball or force turnovers. An integral part of most full and half-court presses, its use as a full-time defensive strategy is limited by its personnel requirements and the fact that putting two guards on one forward leaves the rest of the offense with a three-on-two situation if, indeed, the trap does not contain the ball.

The first step in combatting trapping zones is to keep the ball out of the corners, because the corners are where the traps are most effective. They are especially effective when a forward has dribbled to the baseline and stopped. When she turns to pass the ball, two guards cover her, leaping, shouting, waving their hands wildly to distract her. The results are often as predictable as when insects wander into spider webs.

The guards will try to force the dribbler into the corner by overguarding, but the forwards should strive diligently to resist the temptation to dribble to the baseline and stop.

The second step is to pass the ball quickly. When the ballhandler is double-teamed in the corner, the only other forward likely to be open is the offside high post (Diagram 42), and the dangers of long, high crosscourt passes are too obvious to be dwelt upon, especially since the passer will probably be unable to see clearly where she is passing the ball.

If the ball is passed quickly, however, the defense will not be able to effect the double-team, and even if they do, their movement will leave them out of position to guard the other areas of the court, particularly the offside corner of the free throw line. The defense will *never* allow the inside pass. To hope that they will is tantamount to believing in the Tooth Fairy.

With two guards on the ball and a third protecting against the inside pass, the fourth guard has the choice of defending against the outside pass on the ballside of the court, or giving up the crosscourt pass. Of the two,

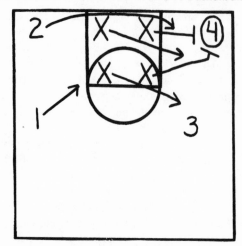

Diag. 42 Trapping The Ball In The Corner, With Offensive Adjustment

she will almost surely opt for the shorter of the two passes, the one to the outside forward on the ballside. The crosscourt pass is dangerous only when the ball is dribbled to the corner and then held, or when the corner forward is a poor ballhandler. A team with proficient ballhandlers should be able to handle the corner double-teaming by looking for the open forwards *before* the trap closes.

Few girls' teams dare to double-team outside, except as part of full or half-court presses. Failure to steal or tie up the ball almost always results in a three-on-two advantage for the offense, and even coaches who like to gamble on defense are reluctant to accept such odds.

THE TRIANGLE-ONE COMBINATION ZONE DEFENSE

There is only one combination zone defense in girls' basketball, the triangle-one. It is basically used against teams having one outstanding forward whose chief attribute may be extraordinary outside shooting ability or ballhandling skill. Sometimes it can upset the tempo, and/or style of that forward's play to the extent that the entire team's offensive efforts are disrupted.

The triangle-one combines zone defense with player-to-player coverage. The zone part of the defense may be either 1–2 or 2–1, while the player-to-player coverage is deployed against the best offensive forward. It is most effective when the opponents have only one outstanding forward who plays outside. It is least effective when the opponents have a balanced scoring attack, or when the best forward sets up low or scores inside. (Diagrams 43–44)

Diag. 43 Triangle-One Matchup With "One" Outside

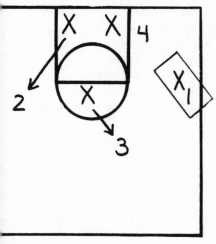

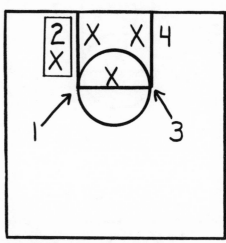

Diag. 44 Triangle-One Matchup With "One" At Low Post

In the first case, with the forward being guarded one-on-one setting up or playing outside, the defensive responsibilities are readily detected, and the *offense* receives most of the pressure. The outside forward may penetrate past the guard defensing her, but she still has the triangle to deal with.

On the other hand, the defensive tasks are magnified when the player-to-player defense involves an inside forward. They must either match up player-to-player with the inside forward—obviously an undesired matchup, since they could have played either player-to-player defense or a matchup zone for a desired single coverage—or double-team her. Of the two, double-teaming will seem to be the most likely choice as explained above, and the other forwards, having a one player advantage, should be able to split the zone for clear fifteen feet shots.

Returning to the problem posed by the outside player-to-player coverage, one way to neutralize the effects of the player-to-player aspect of the defense is to isolate the ''one'' and her guard away from the ball and overload the other side. (Diagrams 45–46) The play then is either for the open shot from the overload, or a pass back across to the isolated forward when the defense matches up one-on-one.

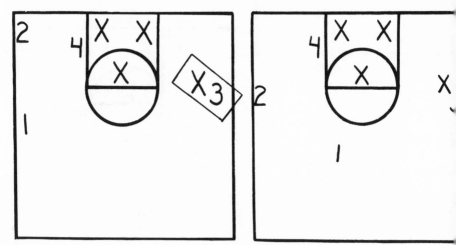

Diag. 45–46 Overloads Away From The Ball Against A Triangle-One Zone

Admittedly, these maneuvers will not succeed when the other forwards are poor shooters and the guards' matchups prevent crosscourt passes to the isolated forward. The best one can do, however, is investigate possibilities, not absolute guarantees. The only "sure thing" in basketball is that there are no sure things. If a team's personnel is such that the loss of one player will devastate that team's playing patterns and chances of winning, special defenses like the triangle-one will likely be successful whatever the offensive strategy.

However, much of the success of the triangle-one often is due, not so much to the defense, but to the exaggerated efforts of the offensive team's premier forward to maintain her normal game in an abnormal situation. Rather than contriving special offenses to utilize the fourth forward, who will still be guarded player-to-player anyway, the offense might isolate the "victim" away from the ball, advising her to look for her shots whenever and however she can, while the others attempt to split the triangle zone for clear shots.

There are other alternatives. First, she might be set at the low post, regardless of her size, especially if her ballhandling abilities are such that she could score inside against a single matchup. Second, she could be utilized in screens such as the crisscross shown in Diagram 34, or the give-and-go. (see "The Four-Player Weave" in Chapter Two) Finally, she could be the object of screens to free her for shots or create unfavorable matchups inside like the simple screen-and-roll in Diagram 47.

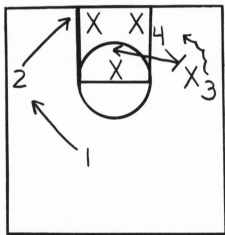

Diag. 47   Screen-and-Roll Against Triangle-One Zone

The special defenses provide no defensive panacea. Whether double-teaming inside, trapping in the corners, or matching up all over the court, each of the special defenses involves considerable risk to the defensive team. These risks might not be readily apparent, but they exist nevertheless, and the team that can maintain a calm mien in the face of aggressive defense can attack those weaknesses.

2
Player-To-Player Patterns

ANALYZING THE DEFENSE

Once upon a time in the relatively brief history of girls' basketball there was only one kind of player-to-player defense, and only one or two offensive options existed against that defense. The guards followed the forwards wherever they went, and the forwards either drove for the basket or took outside shots. If a forward was prevented from driving or taking her outside shot by close defense, she either backed up a few steps to shoot from farther out, or passed to a teammate and cut toward the basket, hoping to break free for a return pass. The scoring was low, and the defense had most of the advantages.

With the discovery and subsequent improvement of screening techniques, and later to an even greater extent with the development of the jump shot as an offensive weapon, the offensive phase of basketball became more versatile, thereby requiring a similar versatility from the defense. As scoring increased coaches saw the need for variations of the original "man-to-man" defense, and the resulting refinements have reached the point where it is not enough to know that a team is in a player-to-player defense. One must also identify the *kind* of player-to-player coverage a team is using. The four types of player-to-player defenses are *sinking, trapping, switching,* and *pressing,* and the examination of each reveals that only certain aspects of a given player-to-player offense will work against any of the four.

Sinking Player-To-Player Defense

The objective of this defensive technique is to give added protection under the basket while enjoying the advantages of one-on-one coverage elsewhere. It usually involves one or more guards away from the ball dropping off their forwards to help out inside, and it is most effective against offenses in which only one or two players figure prominently in scoring or movement of the ball inside.

The best plan of attack against sinking defenses is to keep the guards moving (e.g., by using a continuity offense), and to take the reasonable perimeter shots. The sinking defense is excellent against teams with one tall forward who does most of the scoring, but its value is somewhat limited against balanced attacks in which each forward must be considered a scoring threat.

Trapping Player-To-Player Defense

Trapping usually occurs on a player-to-player basis as a "defensive automatic" when outside forwards cross or attempt to screen-and-roll. It is a risky maneuver, but with fundamentally sound defensive personnel it is a formidable defense. It is strongest against weave patterns, splitting the post, and screens, or situations in which two or more forwards are in close proximity. Conversely, it is weakest against isolation patterns such as clearouts, or continuity patterns (e.g., the shuffle or wheel), where screens and movements occur away from the ball.

Switching Player-To-Player Defense

While trapping defenses are intended to double-team the ballhandler, switching defenses attempt to transfer the guards' defensive assignments whenever the forwards cross or screen. Its strength is the simplification of the defensive techniques by making all switches automatic, and it cuts down on the number of fouls caused by fighting through screens.

In order to attack a switching defense, it is often necessary to turn to the automatics of player-to-player offenses, since the defense's automatic switches are designed to thwart the offense's original intentions.

Pressing Player-To-Player Defense

The basic premise underlying pressing defenses is that when each guard defenses as closely as possible all over the court (fighting through screens and picks when her forward has the ball and trying to keep her from getting the ball when she does not have it), the forwards will be forced out of their regular offensive patterns. The pressing defense is most effective against poor ballhandlers or teams with little offensive movement who depend primarily upon outside shooting. It is not nearly as effective against good ballhandling, players who operate well in one-on-one situations, or offenses involving screens and picks.

ISOLATING FOR ONE-ON-ONE SITUATIONS

Not all offensive maneuvers directly involve all of the forwards. In the most elementary patterns, for example, three of the forwards merely set up or move away from the fourth player, who goes one-on-one against her guard.

In cases where the desired confrontation involves an inside forward, she merely sets up low or breaks into or across the lane to receive the pass, while the other forwards set up two or three steps farther outside than usual. The outside forwards should be discouraged from moving into the basket area, thus bringing their guards with them, while the inside forward is at the low post. Instead, they might run a pattern to occupy their guards and decrease the chances of one or more guards dropping back to double-team the inside forward. A variation of this type of offense involving a high post and outside weave appears later in the chapter as ''The Three-Player Weave''.

This offense works best against pressure player-to-player defense, but it should also be successful against all other player-to-player coverages except the *sinking* type.

A second type of isolation offense is the *clearout*. Used primarily to free an outside forward to go one-on-one, it involves getting the ball to the intended forward, then moving away from the ball in such a manner that three forwards are on the side of the court opposite the ball. These forwards should have something to do when they reach the other side besides standing idly watching the ballhandler perform. They can rotate, set real or imaginary screens, or run a simple weave pattern, but they should not be allowed to stop and watch the action. Even weak defenders will have enough presence of mind to double-team the ballhandler if they, too, are allowed to stand and watch the play unfold.

A simple way of effecting a clearout is shown in Diagram 48. O1

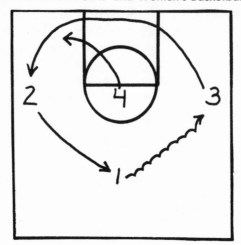

Diag. 48   Simple Clearout For O1

dribbles diagonally to her right and, as O3 and O4 begin their clearing movement to the other side, O1 begins her move toward the basket. She should not wait until they are gone, but move simultaneously with them.

Clearouts may occur from practically any offensive pattern, but their movements are always the same. One forward stays with the ball on one side of the court, while the other three forwards clear to the other side. The second and third movements in the shuffle offense described later constitute a clearout. (The reader is referred to Diagrams 65–66.)

CONTINUITY OFFENSES

Continuity offenses are those offenses in which the movements designed to yield baskets, also permit the forwards to repeat the pattern without moving back to their original positions when no shot is taken. At the end of the pattern, that is, each of the original positions will be filled, although not necessarily by the original forwards.

Continuity offenses consist of set plays followed by movements preparatory to repetition of the pattern. As such, their primary goal is to score points, and the continuity occurs only as an afterthought. The chief advantage of continuity offenses over set plays is that the constant repetition of the pattern keeps the defense moving and tends to lull the guards into automatic switches as they anticipate the forwards' movements. Set plays may yield few or many baskets, but the continuity affords additional scoring opportunities via the offensive automatics.

The three principal types of continuity offenses are the weave, the shuffle, and the wheel. While patterns may vary, it should be safe to say that the difference between them is that weaves involve outside patterns and action near the ball, while most shuffle and wheel movements occur inside and away from the ball.

The Four-Player Weave

Although not generally used as such, the weave pattern can be used as a continuity offense. Most coaches use only parts of its pattern in their offenses, possibly because if it is run correctly the offense will earn a layup or short jump shot off the initial movements. Its efficacy lies in the fact that it consists entirely of basic maneuvers such as the give-and-go and screen-and-roll. Furthermore, like the shuffle and wheel, it gives each player opportunities for movement and scoring from both patterns and free-lancing.

As shown in Diagram 49, the forwards line up 2–2. For explanatory

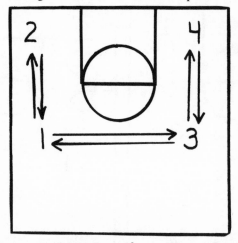

Diag. 49   Basic Four-Player Weave Pattern

purposes, O1 and O3 set up outside, and O2 and O4 are the inside forwards at the low post position on either side of the lane. The numbers O1, O2, etc., refer to the basic positions, or to whatever players occupy those positions. Thus, if O1 and O3 crisscross outside, they assume the number of their new position, with O1 becoming O3 and O3 becoming O1.

Plays are usually called by the ballhandler. It is important from the standpoint of continuity that each position left by a forward be filled by another forward. It might help to picture the offensive halfcourt not as a rectangle, but as a *horseshoe* in which each forward rotates from position to position toward the ball and beyond, until she reaches the baseline. At that point she turns around and advances in the other direction.

Set plays provide the beginning of the weave continuity. Thus, set play "12" may begin either of two ways, as a give-and-go, O1 passing to O3 and screening for O2, or as a screen-and-roll, O1 passing to O2 and screening out her guard. In both cases, O1 screens and O2 is the beneficiary of the screen. (Diagrams 50–51)

Diag. 50   Weave Pattern "12" (Screen-and-Roll)

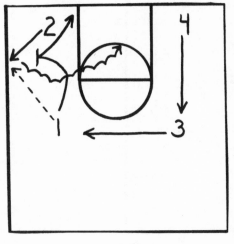

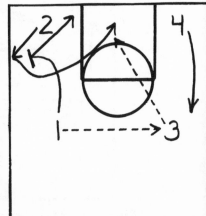

Diag. 51   Weave Pattern "12" (Give-and-Go)

Similarly, "13" may involve O1 passing to O2 (give-and-go), or to O3 (screen-and-roll) before screening for O3. The two plays "12" and "13" are actually *four* different plays. (Diagrams 52–53)

Diag. 52   "13" Give-and-Go

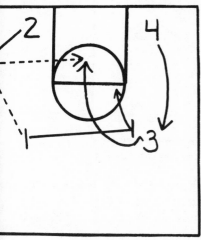

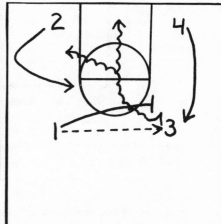

Diag. 53   "13" Screen-and-Roll

A clever variation of "13" is the placement of O4 at high post and sending O1 through as a cutter after the pass to O2. O3 moves across to receive the pass from O2, then relays the ball to O1, who has cut behind O4 at the high post. (Diagram 54) The play will almost always yield an open outside shot, or layup, when O3 can get the ball to O1 behind O4's screen. The play is particularly effective because most of the action occurs away from the ball, and O4 does not have to be particularly talented at screening. O1 merely moves around her.

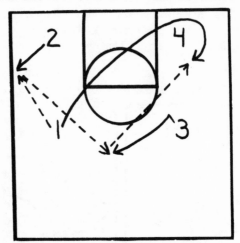

Diag. 54   Backdoor Screen For O1

When O3 initiates the action from her position, "12" becomes "34", and "13" becomes "31". Note that the forwards on both sides of O1 or O3 break outside to receive the pass that initiates movement, whether or not they actually receive the pass. Although making the task of screening slightly more difficult, the movement away from the guard to receive the pass will ensure that the pass is completed.

From the basic give-and-go or screen-and-roll, it is a simple matter to weave into a four-player continuity. As O1 moves to screen for O3 in "13", for example, O2 moves to fill O1's position, and when O3 moves around the screen, O4 fills O3's position. When the guards switch, blocking O3's path, she merely passes to O2 moving toward her. If O2 is not open, she can pass to O4 coming across from the O3 spot, etc.

A problem that often occurs in connection with weave patterns is that of players who simply do not possess the necessary skills to dribble lefthanded, especially at the junior high level. For such players, a variation of "13" (Diagram 55) can be helpful. After passing and screening for O3, O1 continues low to screen for O4. O3 takes one or two lefthanded dribbles and, if overguarded, pivots and drives to the basket righthanded. Of course, if the guards switch, she can pass to O4 moving toward her.

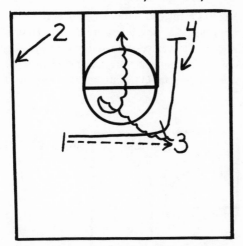

Diag. 55 "13" With Reverse Pivot

Two often-used variations involving O1 are ''14'' and ''134'', in which O1 sets *two* screens.

In ''14'', (Diagram 56) O1's movement is similar to the give-and-go described earlier in Chapter One, in the section of attacking the 2–2 zone

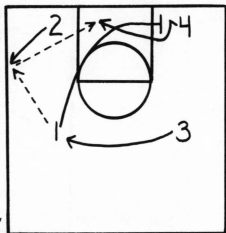

Diag. 56 "14"

defense. (cf. Diagram 7) Instead of rotating, however, O1 screens for O4, who breaks across the lane for the return pass and layup.

"134" (Diagram 57) involves two screens. O1 passes to O2, then screens for O3, who does not penetrate inside the lane if she is not open. O1 continues low to screen for O4, who moves across the lane to receive O2's pass.

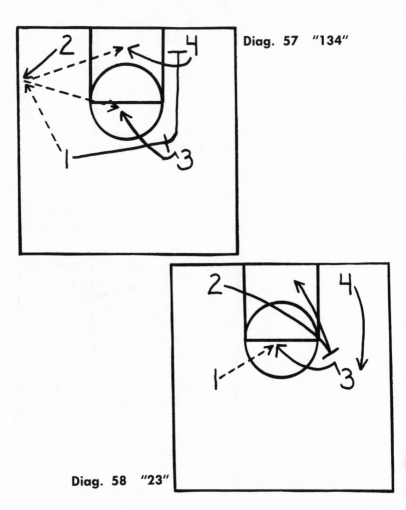

Diag. 57 "134"

Diag. 58 "23"

Actually, the only part of "134" that differs from "13" is the stopping of O3 outside if she is not clear, because O1's continuity involves screening for both O3 and O4 anyway. Resulting variations are seen in Diagrams 58–60.

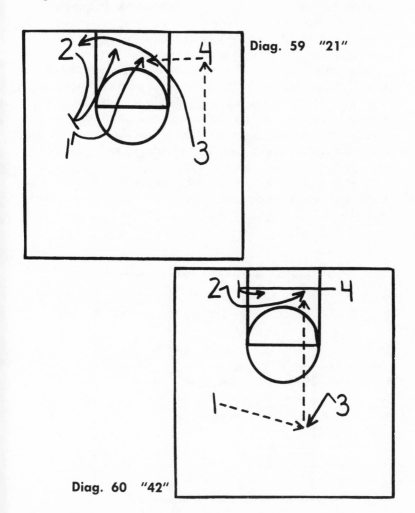

Diag. 59 "21"

Diag. 60 "42"

The Three-Player Weave

One of the most basic of all basketball patterns is the figure-8, or three-player weave. Thought of primarily as a warmup or practice drill, it can also provide a devastating attack against a player-to-player defense, once one has conquered the sticky problem of what to do with the fourth forward.

If she is drastically unskilled, she can be isolated on one side of the court while the continuity is run on the other side. Soon, however, the defense will realize what is happening and will move her guard back to help block the inside pass or drive. Therefore, a team with one unusually weak forward is probably better served by making her a part of the continuity. The unskilled player will usually understand and accept such actions if she is made aware that her responsibilities have not been diminished, indeed, that they also lie in rebounding, screening, pressing, etc.

However, any team with three average forwards and one inside scoring threat or outstanding ballhandler should consider using the three-player weave as a player-to-player offense.

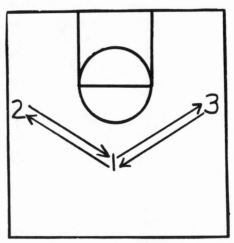

Diag. 61   Rotation In The Three-Player Weave

Play begins with the outside weave. In running the pattern, timing and execution should be stressed rather than speed, since improper timing or sloppy execution will cripple the offense more seriously than good defense.

The positioning of the post player is optional. If her best shot is a turnaround jump shot, she may be most effective at the low post. If she handles the ball or drives well, she can set up at high post at the center or corner of the free throw line.

Whatever the case, set plays off the continuity are keyed on the pass to the post. After the pass, either wing can go backdoor for a return pass and layup (Diagram 62), the post player can drive, or two of the outside forwards can split the post. (Diagram 63)

Diag. 62 Backdoor Movement From Outside Weave

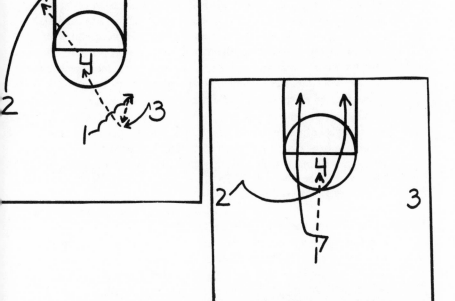

Diag. 63 Splitting The Post From Outside Weave

The backdoor play is particularly effective when executed by the wing opposite the side from which the ball was passed inside, since many guards tend to watch the ball rather than watch their forward. At the moment when the guard turns to watch the ball, the forward breaks behind her to the basket.

If the guard does not make the mistake of watching the ball, she can still be brushed off on the post in the scissoring move of splitting the post.

The usual procedure of splitting the post is for the passer to make the first cut, followed by one or both of the other forwards. When the ball is passed in from the point, both wings may split the post after the point forward's cut. When the ball is passed inside from a wing position, it is customary to use only that wing and the middle forward as cutters, with the wing cutting first. The other wing either goes backdoor as previously described, or continues around outside as a safety valve in case the high post has some trouble passing or maintaining possession of the ball.

Just as faking toward the ball should precede the break to the basket in backdoor plays, the opposite maneuver should be successful when the opponent is not overguarding. In order to ensure being open to receive the pass, the wing forwards should fake a backdoor move, then break toward the ball or outside. Because the objective of the three-player weave is to spread the defense to facilitate the pass into the post, rather than merely running outside figure-8's, it is suggested that the opposite wing delay her move until the pass is made. The transfer should occur preferably on either side of the court midway between the center and the wings, and should not be made at the center of the court, an area unfavorable for passing in to the post.

The heart of the offense is the inside play afforded by the pass to the high post. If she elects to work the ball inside herself rather than passing to a teammate, she needs only a minimal repertoire of shots and moves toward the basket to be a potent scoring threat. A girl who can drive either way or shoot a hook shot or turnaround jump shot can be devastating in this player-to-player offense when the other forwards continue their outside movements after the ball has been passed inside.

If, however, the forwards stop to watch the post operate, the guards will likely seize the opportunity to drop back and help out on defense. To avoid this, the forwards must not stop their weaving movements except to split the post or go backdoor. They should run their weave pattern until they are overguarded, in which case they should automatically break to the basket, or when the ball is passed inside. Even in the latter case, however, the forwards do not have to break their weave pattern. If their post player is sound fundamentally, they probably should not anyway.

Automatics Of Weave Offenses

The first automatic off the weave pattern is the backdoor move of the wings, or the post if she is overguarded. This move is effected by faking a movement toward the ball and breaking directly to the basket. It is important because the defense will try to break up the weave in one of two ways, by overguarding the forward receiving the pass or by overguarding the dribbler to force her toward the middle of the court, and away from the opportunity to pass the ball.

A second automatic, then, is the reverse pivot and drive by the dribbler when she is overguarded in an attempt to break up the weave. She should be open at least as far as the free throw line, since the act of overguarding takes her guard out of the play.

A third automatic is the post's clearing to the side opposite the ball whenever an outside forward breaks the pattern spontaneously to drive to the basket.

A fourth automatic is the screen-and-roll by the passer when the receiver is overguarded after the guards switch. In order to be ready to roll to the basket, the forwards should be taught to watch the ball continuously while running their weave pattern. Indeed, none of the automatics of any continuity offense will succeed unless the forwards are alert for their possibility arising.

A fifth automatic specifically concerning the four-player weave is that whenever one forward cuts to the basket with the ball, the next forward in line, coming from the other direction, cuts behind her, thereby becoming a safety valve passing outlet if the driver's movement to the basket is stopped. (Diagram 64)

A variation of the above pattern is the screen-and-roll toward the basket and across the lane, when the ball is in the corner. Explained earlier as set play ''12'' in the four-player weave pattern, it should be an automatic when it arises, although it affects the weave continuity.

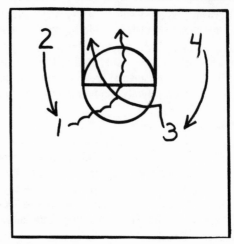

Diag. 64   Scissoring Movement Off Drive In Weave Pattern

The Shuffle Offense

Originally designed for boys' basketball by Bruce Drake of Oklahoma University, and popularized by Joel Eaves at Auburn University, a modified shuffle offense can provide a sound, diversified offensive attack for girls' basketball.

Advantages of the shuffle offense include:

1. It does not depend upon one player, especially a tall forward, for its success. The entire offense is involved;

2. It works against all player-to-player defenses, although a sinking or switching defense will cause it more trouble;

3. It provides opportunities for each forward to score from high-percentage positions; and

4. It provides opportunities for scoring from patterns and free lancing.

The pattern, Diagrams 65–66, starts with O1 handling the ball. O2 breaks outside to receive her pass. After passing to O2, O1 runs her guard into O3 and breaks toward the basket for a return pass. This is the first shooting option, and O1 should be coached to run the pattern correctly, and not merely be rushed haphazardly by O3.

Diag. 65 Basic Girls' Shuffle Movement

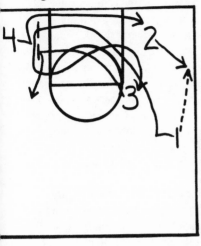

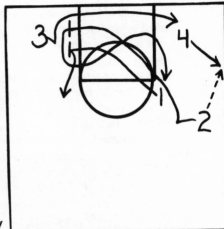

Diag. 66 Shuffle Continuity

If O1 does not receive the pass, she continues on to the other side of the lane to set a screen low for O4. O3 follows to make it a double screen. O4 remains still until both forwards are set, then fakes either way around the screen and goes the other to receive the pass, shooting option #2.

If O4 does not receive the pass, she continues out of the lane and toward the corner. O1 then breaks around O3's screen into the center of the lane for O2's pass, shooting option #3. If O1 does not receive the pass, she continues across the lane to become the new high post.

As soon as O1 goes around her into the lane, O3 breaks out to the corner of the free throw line for O2's pass, shooting option #4. If she does not receive the pass, she returns to low post opposite the ball.

Thus, although not occupying their original positions, the forwards are in position to run the offense again. O4 has assumed O2's original position, O3 has become O4, O1 is now O3, and O2, with the ball, is in O1's spot, ready to pass and break around the high post's screen. After running through the entire pattern four times, each of the forwards will have played all four positions and returned to her original position. The shuffle can be run from either side of the court.

It is readily apparent that the team who uses the shuffle needs good ballhandlers. Much of the threat posed by the shuffle is the fact that all of the players have equal scoring, screening, and ballhandling opportunities, thereby giving the defense no leeway where "weak" guards are concerned.

Still, the shuffle is not an easy offense to run. Players must constantly be urged to work on timing, not speed, and to look for the automatics brought about by defensive adjustments. The screens must be set quickly, but carefully, in order to avoid offensive fouls. Recipients of screens must endeavor to rub off their guards onto the screens every time and, then, be ready to receive the pass. If any of the above are ignored or bypassed, the shuffle movement is likely to bog down under automatic switches by the guards.

By far, the most difficult part of the shuffle is the ballhandling by O2 in Diagram 65. She must not only work free to receive the pass from O1, but, also, must be able to control the ball while dribbling and watching the offensive movements unfold. Finally, she must be able to make a quick, sure pass to her teammate inside at the precise moment when she is open. Even a second's delay in getting the ball to her can cost the team a basket.

Although speed is only secondary to timing in executing the shuffle movements, it *is* important. If O1 or O3 waste time in cutting to set their double screen after the outlet pass to O2, for example, or if the cutters fail to move swiftly along their routes, O2 is likely to be called for a five-second violation, resulting in a held-ball.

Because of the likelihood of the guards using a switching player-to-player defense to combat the shuffle, it is imperative that the forwards familiarize themselves with the automatics of the shuffle offense. They include those movements that can yield layups or short jump shots when the guards switch defensive assignments after each screen-and-cut.

Automatics Of The Shuffle

The first automatic off the shuffle is O2's backdoor option. When the guards realize that the shuffle will not occur until the pass is made to O2, they are likely to overguard O2 to prevent the pass. That being the case, O2 should fake toward the ball, then break for the basket.

The second automatic is for O2 to drive when she is overguarded after she receives the pass. Whenever this happens, all other forwards should immediately clear to the side of the court away from the ball. Stated simply, the second automatic demands that the *forwards should drive at every opportunity,* and its corollary is, *whenever unscheduled drives occur, everyone else clears that side and the lane immediately, regardless of where they are supposed to go.*

The third automatic involves O3's screen for O1 after the pass to O2. If the screen is well executed, O1 will have a layup, except when the guards switch. In this case, O3 will have the layup as O1 clears ahead of her. The offense should not ignore this possibility.

The fourth automatic involves the double screen and ensuing movements. When O4 goes around the screen, the guards will switch, with the guard on whatever side of the screen O4 goes around picking her up. (Diagram 67)

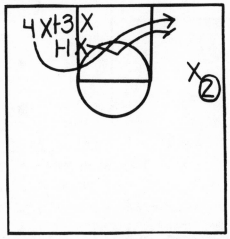

Diag. 67 Defending The Double Screen, First Switch

O1 will still have position on O4's original guard, however, and when *O1* cuts next instead of *O3,* O3's guard will also have to switch. (Diagrams 68–69)

If O2 is alert for momentary openings, and if O1 and O3 are equally alert to the defensive switches, they can reverse the order and/or direction

Diag. 68 Fourth Automatic, 1st Option

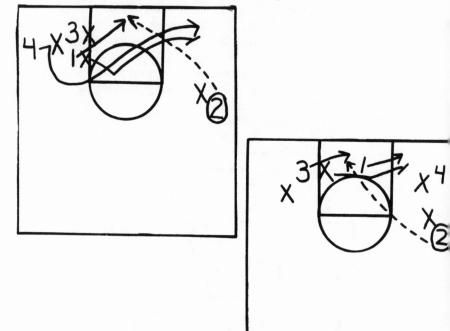

Diag. 69 Fourth Automatic, 2nd Option

of their cuts to give themselves layups that were not even in the movement as it was originally planned.

In addition to the shuffle, many set plays can be formulated from the basic shuffle alignment. These options can help to keep the defense honest, and to provide additional scoring opportunities for selected forwards.

As with the 2–2 zone offense, the set plays are numbered to refer to screeners and cutters, as in "34", where O3 screens for O4, "24", "32", or any of several other combinations. These are seen in Diagrams 70–78.

Diag. 70 Shuffle Clearout

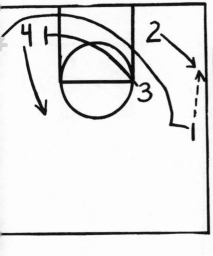

Diag. 71 Screen-and-Roll After First Cut

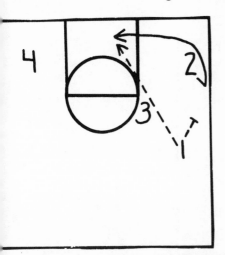

Diag. 72 Shuffle Backdoor Movement

Diag. 73 Screen-and-Roll Before First Cut

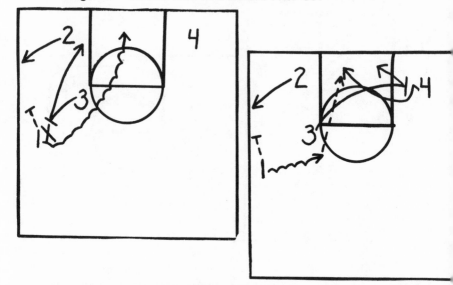

Diag. 74 Set Play "34" From Shuffle

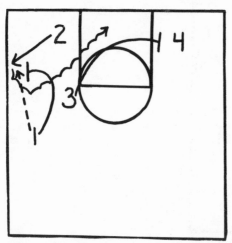

Diag. 75 Set Play "12" From Shuffle

Diag. 76   Double Screen For O2

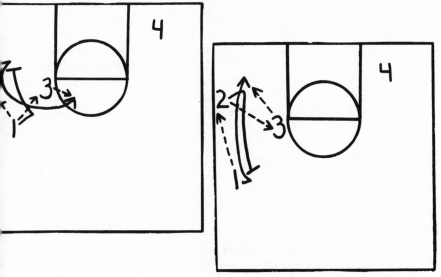

Diag. 77   Double Screen For O1

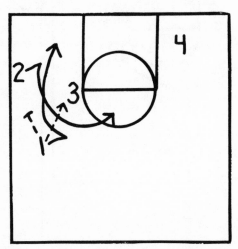

Diag. 78   Splitting The Post

The Wheel Offense

The wheel offense, originated by Garland Pinholster at Oglethorpe University, constitutes a third type of continuity offense capable of modification for girls' and women's basketball. Like the shuffle, the wheel emphasizes patient ballhandling, high-percentage shot selection, and movement away from the ball. The basic wheel alignment is shown in Diagram 79.

The first movement is O4 cutting behind O3 to receive O1's pass. If the defense fails to adjust to this movement, O4 either shoots or drives around O3 in a basic screen-and-roll pattern.

After passing to O4, O1 moves away from the ball to screen for O2, who comes to the top of the circle to receive O4's pass. Upon receiving the ball, O2 relays it to O1, who cuts away from the basket to receive the pass. (Diagram 80) O2 drops low to form a double screen with O3 for O4. O4 cuts either way around the screen, setting up low across the lane. O3 moves out to the top of the circle to receive O1's pass.

Diag. 79   Wheel Offense, First Movement

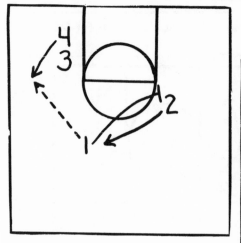

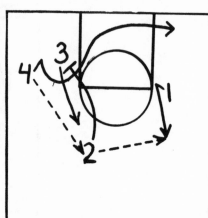

Diag. 80   O4 Cut Off Double Screen In Wheel

In Diagram 81, O1 has passed to O3, then cuts around O4's screen to return to the original wheel positions.

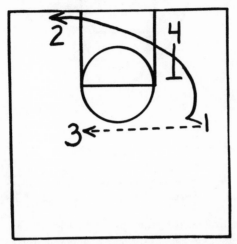

Diag. 81   Backdoor Cut To Reestablish Wheel Pattern

Because the wheel depends to a great extent upon the outside passes, the guards usually attempt to overguard the outlet passes. This disrupts the entire offense unless the forwards are aware of the automatics of the wheel offense. Without automatics, the wheel can literally run down to a stop.

Wheel Automatics

The first automatic off the wheel is the inside fake of O2, and her cut outside to receive O1's pass when O4 cannot get free. O1 then moves inside to set the double screen for O4, thereby eliminating two passes in the pattern.

The second automatic is O4 taking the ball to the basket every time she can after the first pass. O3 should roll to the basket as O4 drives, of course.

The third automatic involves the forward with the ball when she cannot complete the pass to the opposite forward breaking off the screen as shown in Diagram 82. In such cases, the low post on the ballside of the

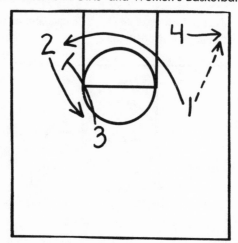

Diag. 82   Second Automatic (Wheel), "Step Out"

court *steps out* to receive the short pass, whereupon the passer cuts to the basket and across the lane to set up a new double screen. The outside forward opposite the ball (O2 in Diagram 82) receives O4's pass, and the original wheel is ready to be run again.

A fourth automatic that sometimes yields an uncontested layup is a reverse and backdoor move around the double screen. This is by O2, after O4 has moved out to receive O1's pass, yielding, in effect, an automatic off an automatic. (Diagram 83)

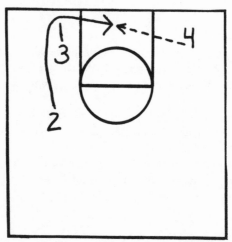

Diag. 83   Fourth Automatic (Wheel), From "Step Out"

As is the case with the shuffle, numerous set plays can be run from the wheel alignment. For example, after passing to O4, O1 breaks down the middle for a return pass. If she does not receive the pass, she veers right and screens for O2, who breaks toward the middle. (Diagram 84)

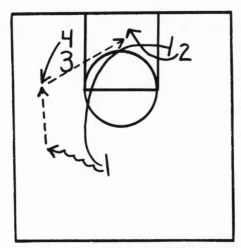

Diag. 84   Set Play "42" From Wheel Alignment

Of course, the single screen for O3 can also provide a double screen for O1 or O2, as shown in Diagrams 85–86. As in the shuffle offense, the

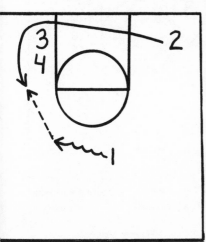
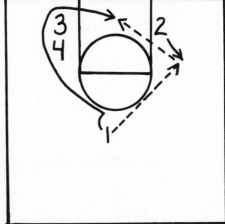

Diag. 85–86   Cutters Off Double Post In Wheel Alignment

success of the double screen depends upon the automatics performed by the screening forwards when the guards switch defensive responsibilities.

Also, the double screen does not necessarily have to be set by the double posts, any forward may do the screening and make the cuts. Two examples are shown in Diagrams 87–88.

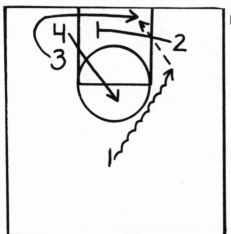

Diag. 87 O3 Cut

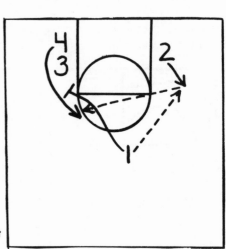

Diag. 88 O4 Cut

In Diagram 87, O3 moves around O4 and continues under the basket as O1 dribbles right. Simultaneous with the dribble of O1, O2 moves to screen whichever guard drops off to guard O3. After O3's cut, O4 drops off to the corner of the lane as a safety valve.

In Diagram 88, O1 passes to O2 and, as O4 breaks around O3 away from the basket, O1 screens whatever guard covers O4.

SET PLAYS

The only real difference between a set play and a continuity pattern is the position of the forwards when they have run through their play without taking a shot. In a set play, they will have to set up again to repeat the play, while in a continuity pattern they will be in position to repeat the play without having to set up.

Actually, set plays consist of placing each of the four forwards at any given spot on the floor, then arranging a sequence of passes and movements that will yield the offense a basket if run correctly. The placement of the forwards depends entirely upon the coach's preferences and available personnel. For example, taller forwards frequently are used at post positions. In addition to the obvious advantage of having offensive height inside, the taller forwards are often used to set screens and picks for the other forwards.

Set plays may be run from practically any offensive alignment, once basics such as individual skills and court balance are taken into account. Concerning court balance, teams may set up as follows: four-out (side); three-out, one-in; two-out, two-in; or one-out, three-in. Obviously, they cannot set up with all four forwards inside. The weaves are examples of four-out and three-out, one-in alignments. The wheel runs from a one-out, three-in setup.

Variations may also occur within the outside-inside alignment. For example, with two-out, two-in, the inside forwards may both line up at low post on the same side, at low post on either side of the lane, one low and one high on the same side, one low and one high on either side, or at the high post on either side.

Because the basic movements of set plays (e.g., give-and-go, screen-and-roll, splitting the post), have already appeared within the

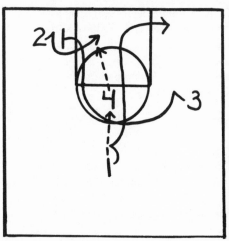

Diag. 89   1–2–1 Alignment

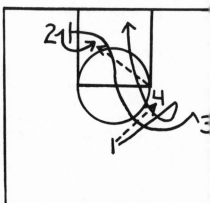

Diag. 90   2–1–1 Alignment

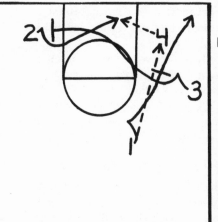

Diag. 91   1–1–2 Alignment

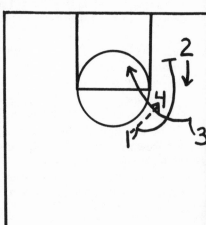

Diag. 92   2–1–1 Alignment

various continuity offenses, four examples of the same play (an outside scissoring movement with inside screen), run from different alignments, should suffice to further exemplify the range of set plays. Note that Diagram 90 contains an additional feature, O1's reverse pivot, in effect giving her two chances to brush off her guard on O4.

3
Special Situations

STALLING

Because of the unfavorable and, to a certain extent, unfortunate, connotations of the term *stalling,* it is difficult to discuss the issue without adding fuel to the already existing arguments concerning the ethics of a team's holding the ball without shooting. However, every successful coach deploys some types of slowdown tactics in certain game situations.

Fans seldom enjoy such tactics, even when used in such harmless situations as holding the ball for the remaining seconds of a quarter in order to ensure that one's own team takes the final shot of the quarter. However, fans are notoriously forgetful about what caused a team to reach the point where a coach might be tempted to use a stalling or delay offense.

While few coaches advocate the wholesale use of stalling offenses, even gamewide deep freezes are not inherently evil. They do not of themselves constitute a menace to the future of the game. Instead, they merely represent a way of playing the game, if and when the coach decides to use them.

The author does not advocate or endorse stalling on a gamewide basis, but feels that two important considerations are often overlooked in discussions of stalling.

First, although stalling is usually associated with basketball, it also occurs in practically every other sport governed by time limits. Second, the coach owes it to his team and its supporters to do everything he can from a coaching standpoint to protect his team's chances of winning, or at least to avoid their being embarrassed by lopsided losing scores.

Two years before this author arrived at his present situation, the girls' team at that school played a particularly powerful neighboring team, losing by the unbelievable score of 94–6. The winners played their starting team almost the entire game, with their leading scorer collecting 23 of her 45 points in the last quarter alone, when her team held a lead of over sixty points.

While basketball purists might struggle for consolation in the fact that the losers did not freeze the ball to keep the score down, it was small consolation to the girls who had to suffer the humiliation of such a crushing defeat. One might also argue that the winning coach acted improperly in running up the score, but such arguments lend support to the contention that stalling is not inherently wrong in *all* situations.

Stalls range from deep freezes, in which a team does not shoot even when presented with open layups; to delays, in which a team takes only the most selective shots; to slowdown offenses, in which the team runs patterns until the desired scoring situation occurs.

Slowdowns

An offense is a slowdown offense when it is used by a team to control the ball, and/or the tempo of the game. This is accomplished via careful ballhandling and shot selection, and constant repetition of the basic pattern. Also called *controlled offense,* this type of slowdown is often seen as a gamewide strategy used against teams with a superior fast break and high scoring potential.

Controlled offenses are not crowd-pleasing in the sense of barrages of high-arching thirty foot field goals or withering fast breaks that produce 100 points per game, but they can keep a team in the game against an opponent who specializes in the above. In their milder forms they merely help to ensure that a team gets a good shot every time downcourt on offense. However, they can also be used to yield the occasional 8–7 scores that raise public outcry for twenty-four or thirty-second clocks.

Slowdowns, then, involve the running clock only as a secondary concern behind getting good shots. Wherever possible, the offense should appear to be the same as the team's regular attack, with emphasis shifted away from random shots, toward such high-percentage shots as layups. Against zone defenses they consist of passing inside or around the zone until the defensive adjustments are acceptable to the offense. Against player-to-player defense it involves repeating the pattern until the defense errs or commits itself. In either case, no shots are taken until the offense has the advantage.

Delays And Freezes

A delay is a partial freeze. The objective of delay offenses is to run the clock while still trying to score when wide open shots occur. A team in a delay offense can be expected to take far fewer shots than they might in their normal offense.

When a team is freezing the ball, they make no effort to score, even when presented with open shots. Except for the game-long deep freezes mentioned earlier, most coaches avoid freezing the ball except to protect a slim lead near the end of a game. Freezing is a dangerous maneuver, and players on the offensive team often become so engrossed in protecting the ball that they forget about everything else. Therefore, this changes the team's attitude from aggressiveness to hesitancy, and it is but a single step from hesitancy to fear.

General Considerations Concerning Delays And Freezes

1. *The best ballhandlers should handle the ball most (or all) of the time.* The wise coach will select or devise a spread offense that will complement the abilities of his players. A team with one good ballhandler should have her handling the ball most of the time, two good ballhandlers should take turns with the ball, etc.

2. *Keep the dribbling to a minimum.* A player should not dribble when she can pass to an open teammate, but in all cases she must **WATCH THAT PASS!**

3. *Avoid crosscourt or other long passes.* When a team holds a lead of only a few points, every pass may mean the difference between winning and losing. The defense hopes to shut off all but the high, arching, crosscourt passes; therefore, the forwards must make every effort to avoid such risks. Additionally, the forwards should be coached to move toward the ball to receive passes, not wait passively for the ball to come to them.

4. *Stay away from the ball.* The greatest hazard to the ballhandler is

double-teaming, and this situation can be avoided by staying away from the ballhandler. Many coaches use offenses that involve cutting away from the ball after each pass. Splitting the post and crossing should be avoided whenever possible.

5. *Keep the ball moving, but keep it out of the corners.* Obviously, the guards' task is made easier when the forwards or the ball are stationary. As long as the ball is moving, the guards must continually make decisions and defensive adjustments, but when it stops, the defense can take the initiative in forcing the action. Also, double-teaming is easiest when the ball is in the corner, because the ballhandler's avenues of escape are more subject to limitation in the corner than elsewhere.

6. *The forwards must run their patterns, except to capitalize on reverse and backdoor plays when overguarded.* It is imperative that the ballhandler knows where all other players on the court are, and where they are likely to go. Any time a guard leaves her forward, as in trapping, that forward should immediately break toward the basket, while at the same time alerting the ballhandler to the situation.

7. *Keep the middle open when freezing the ball.* There are exceptions to this rule, but as a general rule of thumb it is fairly reliable. It negates much of the possibility of defensive double-teaming whenever a forward drives toward the basket. Keeping the pivot open tends to force one-on-one coverage.

ONE-PLAYER DELAYS

Books on coaching basketball seldom deal with one-player delays, primarily because they often lead to a five-second violation or a held ball. Often a team has only one ballhandler skilled enough to protect or advance the ball in pressure situations, however, and delays requiring each forward to protect the ball an equal amount of time simply will not work. To be successful, a one-player delay must have the best ballhandler handling the ball most of the time, while the other forwards cut and screen away from the ball to get free, then pass back to the ballhandler as soon as possible.

Diagram 93 illustrates this basic strategy. As O1 begins her move toward the basket, O2 screens for O4, who receives O1's pass if she is unsuccessful in going all the way to the basket. O1 then breaks away from the basket to receive O4's return pass, begins another move toward the

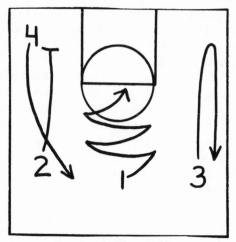

Diag. 93   One-Player Delay (Point)

basket, and O4 screens for O2. O3 moves to the corner and back for movement and diversion.

The weakness of this offense is that the ballhandler must use her peripheral vision and listen for her teammates' warnings of defensive attempts to sink back to double-team her. Because of the difficulty involved in keeping the ball near the middle of the court, many coaches would prefer to keep the ball near the sideline where, although fewer escape routes are available, the ballhandler can see the double-teams before they are sprung upon her.

The basic sideline one-player delay involves isolating the dribbler on one side of the court, while the other three forwards move in some kind of prearranged sequence. In Diagram 94, for example, as O2 begins her move toward the basket, O1 screens for O3, who breaks to the basket for a layup, or, if she is stopped, breaks outside to receive O2's pass. O4 fills O3's position, and O1 continues on to the position of O4. O2 breaks away from her guard, or goes backdoor if overguarded, to receive the pass, and the sequence begins again, this time with O3 screening for O4.

Other screens could be used (e.g., O4 screening for O1 or O3), but the

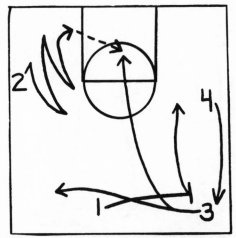

Diag. 94 One-Player Delay (Sideline)

sequence shown in Diagram 94 is likely the best, since O3 has more open court in which to cut and break free of her guard.

Actually, one-player delays are seldom effective. The offensive burden is concentrated too heavily upon one person, and the defense can relax its responsibilities toward the weaker forwards in order to put greater pressure on the others. At the sideline, the defense can use a triangle-one to effectively shut off the cuts to the basket and the outlet pass to the open part of the court. Finally, the one-player offense features dribbling to a greater extent than any other delay, and dribbling is always difficult to maintain against pressing defense.

However, they do have some value, especially to the coach whose second, third, and fourth forwards dribble as if they were wearing boxing gloves and the ball was made of stone.

TWO-PLAYER DELAYS

Generally, *any* delay offense should work as well as a two-player delay if the personnel is arranged properly. For example, the one-player delay can be modified slightly to accommodate two ballhandlers by having the cutter exchange positions with the passer. In Diagram 93, O1 can pass back to O4 after penetrating, then assume her place along the sideline,

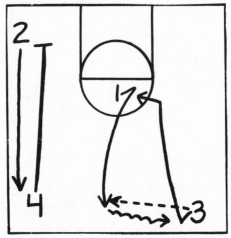

Diag. 95   Two-Player Delay

while O2 returns to her original position and O4 moves to O1's starting point.

The advantages of a two-player delay are that the offense seldom has to risk entrusting ball possession to its lesser skilled ballhandlers, and the defense cannot concentrate its efforts upon a single ballhandler.

In the two-player delay shown in Diagram 95, O1 and O3 take turns handling the ball and cutting for the pass. O4's screen for O2 is diversionary, and contributes no more than movement to hold the other guards' attention away from the ball. O3 holds the ball outside. O1 breaks toward midcourt, or to the basket if fronted, to receive the pass. O1 dribbles right as O3 cuts inside, watching for a defensive lapse by O3's guard. If O3 does not receive the pass, she suddenly reverses and breaks toward midcourt to receive the pass.

It seems that the easiest way to set up the two-player delay is to place them outside and work crossing patterns in a kind of two-player weave. (Diagram 96) Setting the two ballhandlers outside, however, makes the two-player delay extremely difficult to run. In the first place, crossing is a dangerous maneuver at best, with the increased possibility of double-teaming the dribbler; while in the second place, the forwards' cuts must

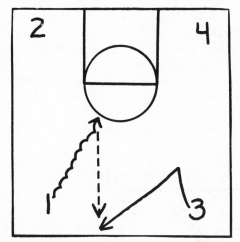

Diag. 96 Two-Player Delay (Outside)

be longer and to more confined areas of the court in order to break free when the layup is cut off.

It can be done, but it is not as easy a maneuver to effect as when one of the two is stationed at high post before breaking. Of course, one can argue that setting the forward at the high post lessens the possibility of the layup, but most girls, however, are taught to give up the outside pass before allowing the layup anyway, so the layup is *supposed* to be a remote possibility in either setup.

Finally, that the two-player delays appear to be inferior to other systems bears repeating. A coach should not spend too much time on such methods, for with slight modifications of the material presented, any of several other team delays may be used.

TEAM DELAYS AND FREEZES

Two types of alignments for delaying or freezing the ball, the 2–2 and 3–1, are seen more often than any others. Both feature the pivot and the free throw lane left open while the offense sets up far outside, but similarities between the two stop at that point. The 2–2 is often used as a delay offense because it affords more opportunities for layups. The 3–1 is more frequently seen as a deep freeze offense because it involves a semi-rotation pattern as opposed to actual cuts to the basket.

The first option with the 2–2 is O3's pass-and-cut to the basket. (Diagram 97) If O3 fails to receive the pass, she can continue around to fill O1's original position—in which case it becomes a two-player delay—or she can cut to her right and set a screen on O4's guard. (Diagram 98) When O4 receives O1's pass, O3 assumes O4's position, and O1 either cuts to the basket or screens for O2. (Diagram 99)

Diag. 97   2–2 Delay (Pass-and-Cut)

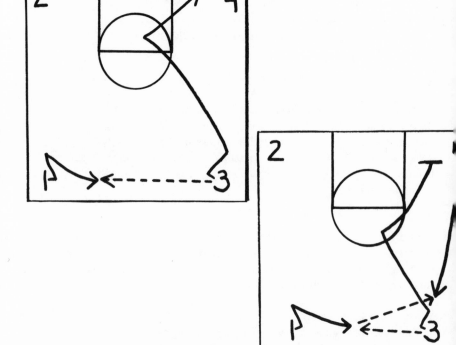

Diag. 98   2–2 Delay (Screen For O4)

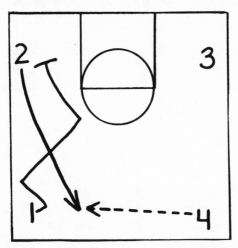

Diag. 99   2-2 Delay, Rotation To Other Side

The movement of the 3–1 offense starts outside near the center of the court, with O3 faking a cut to the basket, then moving toward O1 to receive the pass. After the pass, O1 cuts to the basket and swings around to a position opposite O4 (the "1" in 3–1.) O3 dribbles left as O2 fakes a cut toward the basket, then moves toward O3 to receive the pass. By now O1 has filled O3's position, and O3 will fill O4's spot after cutting to the basket. (Diagram 100)

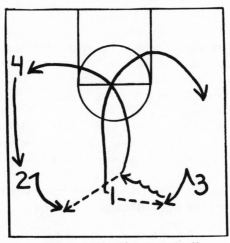

Diag. 100   The 3–1 Stall

The 3-1 is basically an outside weave and, like all other weaves, its success depends upon the familiarity of the players with automatics such as cutting to the basket when overguarded.

BRINGIN PLAYS

Sideline Patterns

Due to the large number of players on the court and the fact that two guards are always present at the offensive end of the court, it is difficult to design scoring plays from any type of sideline bringin. This is especially true of backcourt out-of-bounds situations. Practically the only play leading to a scoring situation from a backcourt bringin, aside from the formation of a three-on-two fast break (explored in-depth in Chapter Four), is a baseball type pass to a deep forward who is isolated one-on-one.

That the defense can shut off the direct scoring opportunities is of little consequence, however, for the offense's primary concern in backcourt bringin situations is usually just to get the ball into play without losing possession via a turnover.

Set plays are not vital to the success of sideline bringins, but certain principles should be adhered to in order to inbound the ball and move it across halfcourt quickly and without wasted effort.

1. *All random movements should be eliminated.* One of the most frequently encountered mistakes among inexperienced players is being able to see an open area and moving toward it before the referee hands the ball to the teammate out of bounds. This ensures that the area will not be open when the inbounds pass is made. Whether or not a set play is used, players should refrain from breaking toward the ball or an open area until the inbounds passer *has the ball in her hands*.

2. *The best ballhandler should be responsible for getting the ball across halfcourt,* whether the pass comes directly to her or to someone else who relays it to her. Another way of saying the same thing is that the poorer ballhandlers should handle the ball as little as possible. An old trick that often works is to have the best ballhandler make the inbounds pass from the sideline, then break toward her basket to receive the return pass and start the fast break. (Diagrams 105, 109)

3. *Every patterned bringin should have contingency cutters,* or secondary receivers breaking in case the primary cutter is covered. The inbounds passer has *five seconds* to get rid of the ball after the referee hands it to her, and she cannot afford to waste time hoping that her intended receiver will break free if covered closely or double-teamed.

A familiar method of lining up for bringins is the "three abreast" pattern, either parallel or perpendicular to the sideline.

In the first pattern (Diagram 101) the players line up parallel to the sideline, as the ends cross and the middle breaks away from the passer. In Diagram 102, the players set up perpendicular to the sideline in an I-formation, while O3 and O5 break to either side and O4 breaks through the opening toward the ball.

Diag. 101 "Three Abreast," Parallel Alignment

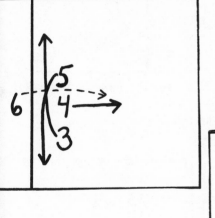

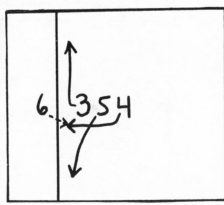

Diag. 102   "Three Abreast," I-Formation

The second pattern can also be reversed, with O3 and O5 breaking away from the ball.

Diag. 103 Variation Of I-Formation Cut

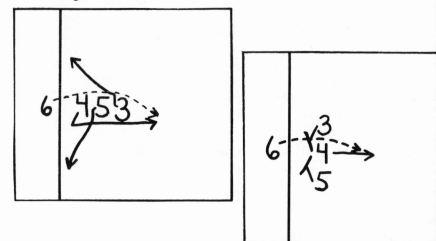

Diag. 104 Double Screen, Sideline Backcourt

Diag. 105 Give-and-Go, Sideline

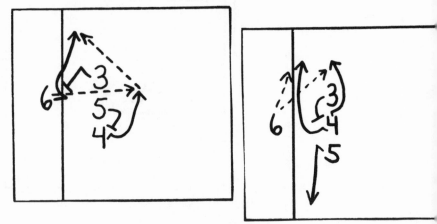

Diag. 106 Backcourt Screen For Downcourt Pass

Diag. 107 Modified I-Formation, Backcourt Sideline

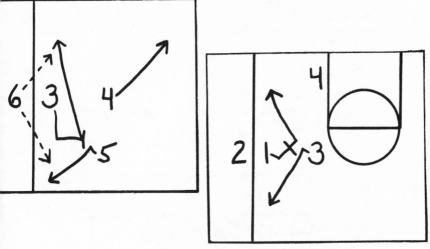

Diag. 108 Forecourt Sideline Bringin

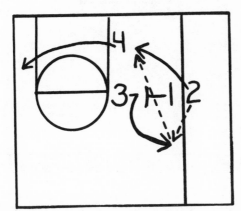

Diag. 109 Forecourt Bringin, Give-and-Go

Other variations of sideline bringin alignments can be seen in the preceding Diagrams 103–109.

BASELINE BRINGIN—FORECOURT BASELINE

With modification, the same alignments and patterns of screening and cutting can be used at the offensive baseline as well as at the sidelines. The following diagrams of bringin plays at the offensive baseline reflect this conclusion.

Backcourt baseline bringin techniques and patterns have been included in the section on full-court presses, and are shown in Diagrams 110–115.

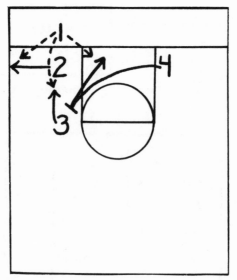

Diag. 110 Baseline Screen-and-Roll

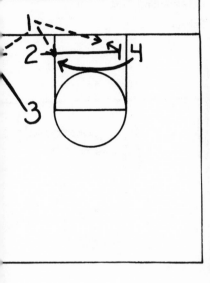

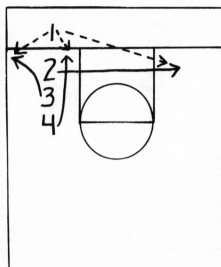

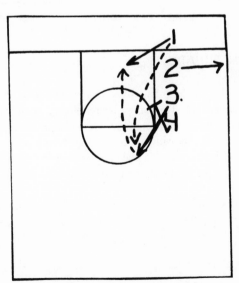

Diag. 113 Baseline I-Formation, Give-and-Go

Diag. 114 Baseline Double Screen

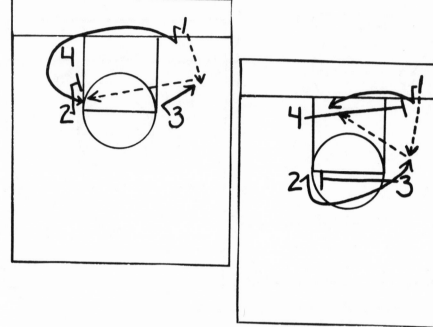

Diag. 115 Baseline Give-and-Go Variation

JUMP BALL SITUATIONS

The objective of jump ball situations is, of course, to gain or retain possession of the ball. This can be accomplished in one of two ways; the jumper can tap the ball to a teammate, or a player can jump in front of an opponent when the opposing jumper controls the tip. Of the two, the latter is far more difficult, since the players cannot change their positions from the time the referee warns them until the ball is touched by a player after the toss.

The players should be made aware of their individual duties before the ball is tossed up by the referees. Players outside the circle should attempt to gain the most advantageous position for their team. If their strategy is to win the tip, they should be positioned so that the jumper has an open space to tap the ball and, if they anticipate losing the tip, they should be where they can stop the fast break or inside shot after the tip.

Also, the player's stance determines to a great extent her ability to protect her position during and after the tip. Her feet should be spread to at least shoulder width, knees bent, with her elbows wide and hands high. In addition to improving balance and agility, this stance gives the jumper a better target at which to aim her tap.

Where the jumper is concerned, the most common error is looking around to see where to tap the ball as the referee begins the toss. The jumper should not prepare to jump until the referee positions the players or warns them not to move. She should use that time to find the open spots, the most desirable places to tap the ball, and she should know where she is going to tap the ball before she steps up to the referee.

There are two common methods of initiating plays in offensing jump ball situations. The first involves *oral* signals which may be given in a variety of ways. The jumper may call out the name of the player to whom she expects to tap the ball, or she can call out the name of the *cutter,* who breaks toward a passing lane or the basket as the ball is tapped to another player.

Another way of calling the offense is by *number.* If a team has several different attacking sequences they may have different play numbers, but few teams have such a diversity of offensive jump ball plays at their disposal. Some teams consider the circle as a giant clock face, and the number that their jumper calls refers to the direction of her tip. For example, "Twelve" would mean "Twelve o'clock" in the direction she faces, so she would tip the ball directly ahead of her. "Three" would be directly to her right as she faces her basket, "six" would be directly behind her, etc.

The second method of initiating plays from jump balls, does not involve signals at all, but is accomplished by keying on the openings afforded by the defensive alignment. It is easily demonstrable that the defense cannot adequately cover both sides of all five nonjumpers, so the offense gears the direction of the tip and subsequent screens and cuts to the defensive setup.

Center Circle Jump Balls

Almost all defenses in jump ball situations attempt to cover the tip directly toward the opponents' basket. Usually this is done by placing guards on either side of their opponents' "Twelve o'clock" position, and by dropping back at least one guard to the free throw line. This alignment is shown in Diagram 116. Diagram 117 depicts a variation of the basic defensive setup sometimes used when a team is almost sure to lose the tip and is slow in dropping back to stop the fast break.

Diag. 116   Basic Alignment For Defensing The Center Jump

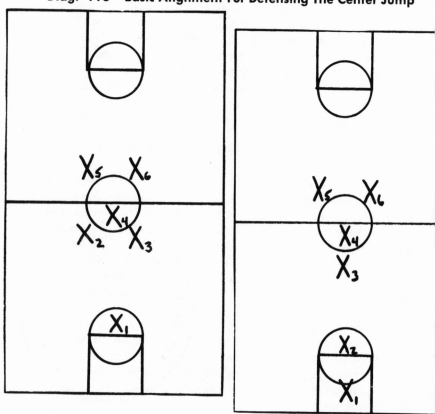

Diag. 117   Variation Of Defensive Center Jump

Against an alignment such as that presented in Diagram 116, set plays may be run to utilize a team's fast break potential. In the first, the ball is tipped to the side of whatever forward has the open spot, and the rover stationed in backcourt cuts behind the forward to receive her pass. The deep forward (O6 in the Diagram) screens the guard, O3 fills the middle lane, and O4 and O5 fill the passing lanes in the fast break. (Diagram 118)

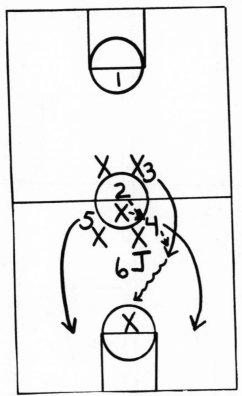

Diag. 118   Fast Breaking Off Center Jump

A variation of the above is to tip to O3, who passes downcourt to O4 losing her guard on O6's screen. O3 then fills the outside passing lane.

Varying the alignment by placing O4 between the guards can also yield favorable results. The ball is tipped to O5, and O6 screens out the guard on that side. O3 and O4 break toward the basket, and O5 passes to O4 for a two-on-one situation or three-on-two, if O6 rolls after screening. O5 can also dribble around O6's screen, with O4 simultaneously screening the other guard at the circle. This allows O5 and O3 to move into a two-on-one situation with the deep guard. (Diagrams 119–120)

Diag. 119   Quick Opener For O4 From Center Jump

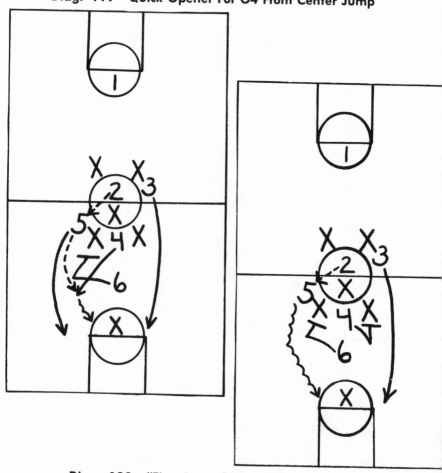

Diag. 120   "Five Around" Fast Break From Center Jump

If the guards line up as shown in Diagram 117, the offense will have little opportunity to fast break, but the task of winning the tip will be greatly facilitated. Such alignments are rare, however.

Backcourt Jump Balls

Any of the previously described methods of offensing the tip will work equally well at a team's defensive circle. The maneuver can be simplified by bringing O6 into the circle between the guards, then having her break straight toward her basket to receive the tip as she is breaking. O4 and O5 fill the outside lanes, with O3 acting as a trailer.

Forecourt Jump Balls

On defense, a team usually tries to cover the tap toward the center of the court, forcing the receiver toward the outside of the court, as illustrated in Diagram 121. If the ball is tapped between O1 and O3, they should be able to double-team the receiver.

If O4 happens to win the tip from this alignment, she should direct the ball toward O3, then pivot and screen the outside guard to allow O3 to drive or shoot from the free throw line. (Diagram 122)

Diag. 121   Forwards Defensing The Tip

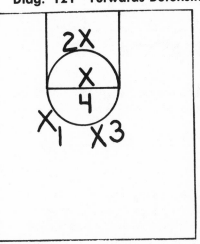
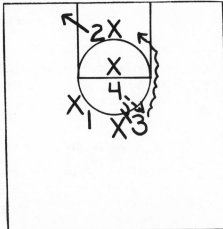

Diag. 122   Offensing A Defensive Tip Situation

When the guards are defensing the tip, they set up with two guards inside and one outside. The easiest method of offensing the tip is to tap the ball to the outside of O2 or O3, depending upon which side of O1 the outside guard lines up. O1 breaks toward the ball, receives the pass, and either shoots if open, or brushes her guard off on O2 or O3 if closely guarded. (Diagram 123)

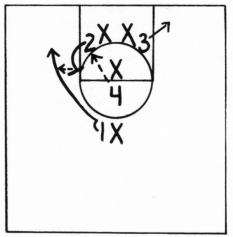

Diag. 123   Forwards Offensing The Tip

In any case, the forwards should have a definite plan of action in mind every time they expect to win the tip, and, if at all possible, that plan should lead to a layup.

FREE THROW SITUATIONS

It is difficult enough to fast break after a successful free throw against a weak defensive team, but it becomes a near impossibility against a strong defense. In the case of missed free throws a team's chances increase, and the situations to be discussed involve the sequence of events and patterns that develop after missed free throws.

Forecourt Free Throws

Aside from isolated instances of outleaping an opponent to rebound a teammate's missed shot, there are few opportunities for creative coaching where offensive free throw situations are concerned. The defense has all the advantages via the inside positions along the lane and if the guards block out properly, the forwards can do little except hope for the ball to take a crazy bounce.

One piece of strategy that sometimes works is that, instead of lining up all of the forwards at the line for rebounding or near midcourt to stop the fast break, a team can position one forward behind either of the rebounders as an outlet for tipping.

When the forward is lucky enough to get her hands on the ball, she often has trouble getting off her shot because the guards are stationed on either side of her in a natural double-team. Positioned out by one, double-teamed by two, her best bet is to try to *tip* the ball rather than catch it. If she is adept at tipping she can try for the basket, but if she is not skilled at tipins, she can tip the ball back to a teammate waiting outside and retain ball possession at the offensive end. (Diagram 124)

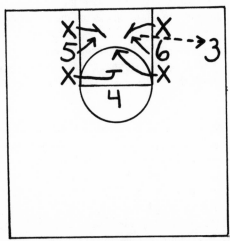

Diag. 124 Tipping A Missed Free Throw To A Teammate

The value of tipping out to retain possession must be weighed against the danger of having the tip intercepted by an opponent, but a surprising number of teams will leave the outside forward unguarded in their urgency to get the rebound.

Another tipout method involving an even more advanced skill is tipping the ball outside to oneself. Not only does that forward have to possess a high degree of tipping ability, but she must also be aware of the location of the other players on both teams, and she must also have the agility to recover the ball after completing the play.

While on the subject of tipping the ball to teammates, we might venture an opinion on the notion of tipping the ball back to the free throw shooter. Forget it! In most cases she is screened out anyway, but there is also the possibility of tipping it too far and helping the opponents start their fast break. Players should thoroughly be coached the rule *if you do not know exactly where you are tipping the ball and who is there to catch it, do not tip the ball: Catch it!*

Free Throws—Backcourt

The basic alignment in defensing free throws is to have two rebounders to block out the inside forwards, a third player to block out the shooter, and a fourth player to receive the outlet pass to start the fast break. Generally, all four guards line up along the lane, with a prearranged signal as to which outside guard blocks out the center and which breaks outside to receive the outlet pass.

If the rebounder passes outside before dribbling, the rover to whom she passes should be clearing to the *side* of the court (#1 in Diagram 125), rather than the middle.

Diagram 126 shows a typical fast break pattern as it develops from the rebound of a missed free throw. After the shooter releases the ball, O5 and O6 step in front of the near forwards and block them out. The rebound comes to O5 who clears outside dribbling, going no farther outside than she has to. She continues to advance the ball, intending to pass to a wing as soon as she is challenged.

Meanwhile, O3 clears to the sideline as soon as it becomes obvious that O5 will claim the rebound, and O4 blocks out the shooter. Both of them,

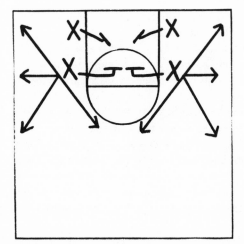

Diag. 125 Blocking Out Inside, Possible Breaking Routes
Outside

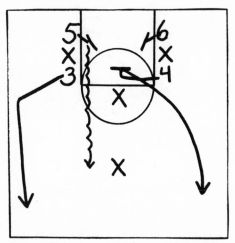

Diag. 126 Rebounder Leading Fast Break

O3 and O4, should not take their eyes off O5 once she gets the ball, because either of them might be clear for the outlet pass.

When O5 begins dribbling downcourt, O4 fills the lane opposite O3, starting the three-on-two fast break. If O5 passes to either of the wings before reaching halfcourt, she drops back. If she dribbles across, one of the rovers drops back.

Fast breaks in which the rebounder dribbles downcourt are not usually as effective as those in which she passes to a teammate already breaking downcourt. The exception is against teams who are slow to get back on defense or weak in stopping the ball. Additionally, the situation described above requires a rebounder who is also a good dribbler. Such situations are often encountered, however, especially at the junior high or high school levels, where one or two good players can carry most of the load offensively and defensively.

When the dribbler chooses to make the outlet pass to the wing as in Diagram 127, the pattern varies only slightly. O3 breaks outside to receive the pass, then dribbles downcourt, or passes to O4 if covered by the safety guard.

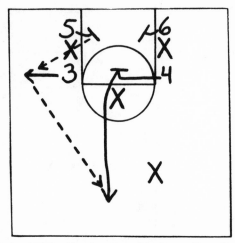

Diag. 127   Outlet Pass To Start Fast Break

A pattern often used by teams with one good, small ballhandler is for the intended ballhandler to break in whatever direction she chooses after a teammate rebounds the missed free throw, and the rebounder passes to her as soon as she finds her. (Diagram 128)

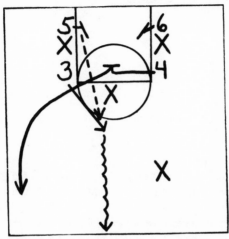

Diag. 128   Direct Pass To Start Fast Break From Missed Free Throw

4
Full-Court Offenses

FULL-COURT PRESSES

General Considerations

1. As soon as the other team scores, if possible, the players should move to their positions and make the inbounds pass quickly, before the defense is ready.

2. The best ballhandlers should bring the ball down court. The easiest way to effect this in the 1–3–2 alignment is to have the best ballhandler at either the wing position on the ballside, or as the inbounds passer. The second best ballhandler should be at the other of these two positions.

3. Long passes and crosscourt passes, especially crosscourt passes, should be avoided except by the most expert of ballhandlers.

4. When no one breaks free for the inbounds pass, the inbounder should immediately call time out.

5. The greatest danger in advancing the ball against presses is defensive double-teaming. The ballhandler should always keep her head up while dribbling in order to spot trapping movements before they arise, and teammates should look for, and move to, openings in the defense.

6. When the offense attempts to force one-on-one coverage, the ballhandler should not begin dribbling until her teammates clear away from her. Once she starts dribbling, she should not stop dribbling until she is ready to pass the ball. Players who catch the ball prematurely can make mediocre presses look good.

7. Dribblers should attempt to take the ball to the middle of the court rather than down the sidelines as a matter of habit. Most double-teaming

situations are geared toward the sidelines, where a player has fewer escape routes available.

Player-To-Player Full-Court Presses

If a team is lucky enough to have one or two decent ballhandlers, the player-to-player presses are the easiest of all full-court defenses to break, once the offense makes the inbounds pass. After the bringin, the other forwards merely spread out far enough to allow the dribbler to maneuver downcourt without being double-teamed. She should then have little trouble getting the ball across halfcourt.

The greatest difficulty encountered in player-to-player press coverage is getting the ball into play. Any of several methods of working the ball inbounds can be employed. A basic bringin alignment against player-to-player defense is the 1–3–2 setup, with the "1" referring to the inbounds passer, the "3" to three forwards spread out across the court in the vicinity of the free throw line, and the "2" to the two stationary forwards. (Diagram 129)

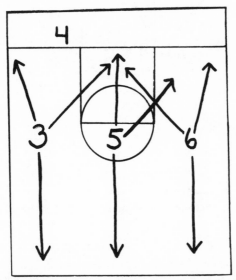

Diag. 129   Basic 1–3–2 Cutting Patterns Against Player-to-Player Coverage

From this alignment, the simplest method of freeing a forward is to have one or more breaking either toward the ball or a corner, or away from the ball or downcourt if overguarded, to receive the pass. In Diagram 129, O3 is the primary receiver, while O5 and O6 are secondary receivers. If O5 or O6 receives the inbounds pass, O4 will break directly toward the receiver for a handoff rather than a pass, especially if she is a weak ballhandler. O3 should wait for the forward to make her assigned movement before starting her dribble.

From the same alignment, a team might prefer to use a screen-and-roll pattern to put the ball into play, with O3 still the primary receiver. (Diagram 130) O3 screens for O5, then rolls diagonally across the lane if the guards switch.

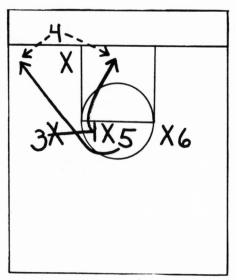

Diag. 130   Screen-and-Roll Off 1–3–2 Inbounds Pattern

Of course, any of the three players lined up along the imaginary extension of the free throw line can screen for any of the others, but the rule of thumb is to have the better ballhandler setting the screen and rolling, since she is then in a more natural position to receive the ball.

Another pattern sometimes seen against player-to-player presses is the "I" formation also used in sideline bringin and baseline bringin plays at the offensive end of the court. It is particularly effective in freeing O3 for the long downcourt pass to start the fast break. O3, lined up in front, nearest to the inbounds passer, waits until O5 and O6 break, then breaks full speed toward midcourt for the pass. (Diagram 131)

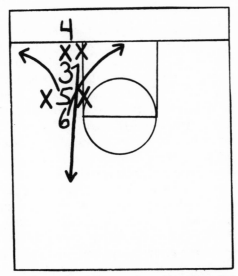

Diag. 131   The I-Formation, Baseline Bringin

The guards can adjust to stop the long pass, but not without opening up some other area for a break. The three guards should not be able to cover all four sides against an alert offense.

Once the ball is successfully inbounded, getting the ball downcourt is simply a matter of avoiding double-teams while advancing the ball. Other forwards should stay away from the dribbler by spreading out to the corners as the dribbler works the ball up the middle of the court, or clearing to the opposite side of the court so the dribbler can come up the sideline. A teammate should act as a safety valve by lagging behind, and away from, the dribbler, or by being prepared to break to the open part of the court if the dribbler encounters difficulty in getting the ball across half-court.

With any kind of effective ballhandling ability, however, a team should experience little difficulty in advancing the ball past midcourt against player-to-player defense.

Zone Presses

2–2–2 FULL-COURT PRESS

The 2–2–2 full-court pressing alignment appears almost universally in girls' and women's basketball. In fact, both the 1–3–2 and 3–1–2 full-court presses usually rotate into 2–2–2's after the ball is inbounded, differing only in the manner of setting up the double-teaming situations.

There are two schools of thought in attacking zone presses. The first is to split the openings, or *seams*, in the zone by sending one or more cutters into that area to receive passes. The other is to spread the defense by placing a forward in each of the four corners, thus forcing one-on-one coverage. Of the two, splitting involves greater risks, but it also yields more fast break opportunities. On the other hand, spreading offers more ballhandling security with less fast breaks. Thus, each has advantages over the other that could dictate their use in certain situations.

With either approach, it is important to take into consideration the goals of the defense. If the guards are content to merely matchup one-on-one, the offense operates under player-to-player principles as explained previously. When the guards attempt to double-team the ballhandler, the forwards must be alert to areas where the splitting patterns should occur as different guards form the double-team.

For example, the double-team may occur in the middle or in the corner after the inbounds pass, as shown in Diagrams 132–133. If the pass is made to O4 in the corner, O3 cuts into the lane, and O5 cuts into the opening between the four guards. If the pass is to O5 in the middle, O3 breaks to the corner, while O4 breaks into the opening between the two guards.

In both patterns above, the receiver is in an ideal position to begin the fast break if the pass is made into the opening. If the pass is not made into the opening, the ball can be passed or relayed to O6 to keep the fast break possibility alive. In any case, if the recipient of the pass beyond the first

Diag. 132 Splitting The Double-Team In The Middle

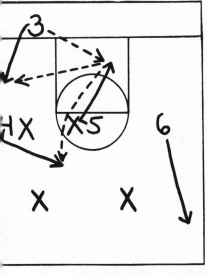 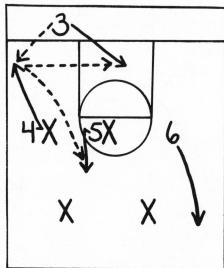

Diag. 133 Splitting The Double-Team In The Corner

line of defenders can *force* X3 and X4 to double-team her, the offense should be able to form the intended three-on-two fast break.

Spreading a zone press refers to the process whereby the forwards force one-on-one coverage by inbounding the ball, then spreading out to the corners. Such an approach is not conducive to fast breaking, except when the guards persist in attempting to double-team despite the spread.

The 1–3–2 offensive alignment is perhaps the most popular in use against full-court presses, especially zones, because it gives a team three players to receive the inbounds pass, instead of just one or two who can be double-teamed.

Effecting The Spread From Various Inbounds Passes

The spreading patterns shown in Diagrams 134–136 are not nearly so difficult as they seem at first glance. They can be taught to junior high

Diag. 134   Passing To The Ballside Wing

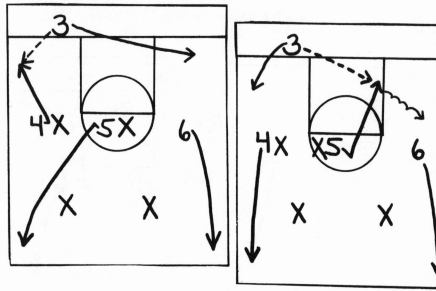

Diag. 135   Passing To The Middle

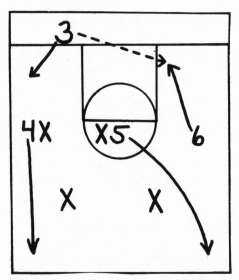

Diag. 136   Passing To The Offside Wing

players rather easily, once they grasp the notion of *keying their movements to the direction of the inbounds pass,* as explained below.

1. *The inbounds passer.* She may pass to any of her three teammates in order to get the ball into play. Concerning players too inexperienced to know when to break, the positions might be numbered, with the inbounds passer calling the number of the desired cutter. Admittedly primitive, this procedure could be effective in certain situations.

Her movements following the pass are dictated by the direction in which she passes. She should always break to the corner *opposite the ball.* If she passes to the middle, she goes to the corner nearest her. She then serves as the safety valve, in case the forwards have trouble advancing the ball beyond halfcourt. When the ballhandler is double-teamed in the opposite corner, she is the most likely candidate for moving the ball downcourt.

2 & 3. *The wings.* The task of the wings is simple. They are to break to the corner to receive the inbounds pass, or to clear to their midcourt corner. Upon receiving the inbound pass the dribbler works her way downcourt one-on-one or, failing to receive the pass, she clears to the midcourt corner on her side. If she receives the pass at midcourt, she should be in a good position to lead the fast break.

The wings are often guilty of a grave error after the inbounds pass. They try to return the ball to the passer before she can clear to the opposite corner. This mistake occurs frequently with young or inexperienced players eager to get rid of the ball before making a mistake. In their haste to escape the pressure situation, they make a blind pass to the inbounder while she is in the vicinity of the free throw lane, rather than waiting for her to clear to the corner. If a defender lurks in that area, she can pick off the pass for an easy layup.

4. *The pivot.* The forward setting up at the high post position in the 1–3–2 alignment is usually the second choice as an inbounds pass recipient, ranking behind the ballside wing. When she receives the pass she either returns the ball to the inbounder and moves to the opposite corner, or dribbles diagonally forward away from the passer's corner, as shown in Diagram 135.

If she does not receive the inbounds pass, the pivot's movement is always to the midcourt corner away from whatever wing receives the pass.

At this point, however, the problem has only been partly solved. After achieving the spread, the offense must still move the ball downcourt without sending a fifth forward across the half-court lines and/or losing the ball in unexpected double-teaming situations while rotating the forwards to maintain the spread.

Although numerous possibilities exist for moving the ball downcourt, the first that comes to mind is dribbling. The direction that the dribbler will go depends primarily upon the defense's trapping techniques and intentions. She may be forced either toward the middle of the court or the sideline, but in either case the general rule holds that the forwards *should stay away from the dribbler*. If the ballhandler dribbles up the sideline as in Diagram 137, O5 should move either across the half-court line or to the middle of the court as shown below. Of the two, the former method is usually preferable, since it permits two cutting lanes for pass receivers rather than one.

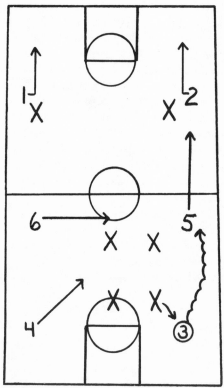

Diag. 137 Dribbling Along The Sidelines Against A Full-Court Press

All methods of beating the full-court presses should include one player with the sole responsibility of staying back and away from the ball as a "safety valve" receiver. This is in the event that the dribbler is stopped and the passing lanes are covered. In Diagram 137, O4 is the safety valve and, if O3 dribbles up the right sideline, O4 will attempt to stay back and in the clear as the opponents double-team the dribbler.

When the dribbler goes to her left toward the middle of the court (Diagram 138), O4 clears to the midcourt corner, and O6, who is already in the corner, clears to the middle of the court—or across the half-court line, if she is a rover. The simplest method of assuring presence of a safety valve in this case is for O5 to drop back as soon as she sees O3 dribbling left.

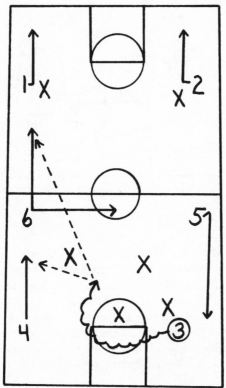

Diag. 138 Dribbling To The Middle Against A Full-Court Press

Regardless of the dribbler's movements, the forwards can simplify her problems merely by staying away from her whenever possible. The dribbler, too, can aid her own cause by (a) anticipating the double-teaming situations, and (b) watching closely the defensive adjustments to the forwards' cutting routes shown in the diagrams.

Possible double-teaming situations involving O3 after the spread is achieved are shown in Diagram 139.

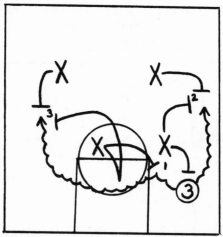

Diag. 139   Possible Trapping Situations In Dribbling Against A Full-Court Press

O3 must wait for the spread to be achieved before beginning her movement. If the guards incorrectly attempt to defense O3 before she moves the ball, she should pass immediately to a free teammate, usually O4 in the opposite baseline corner. When this occurs, O3 becomes the safety valve when O4 dribbles up the left sideline. O6 will leave her corner only when O4 dribbles toward her corner—that is, if O4 starts toward the corner, then pivots to her right and goes down the middle of the court, O6 will cross the half-court line only when she is supposed to be a rover. (Diagram 140)

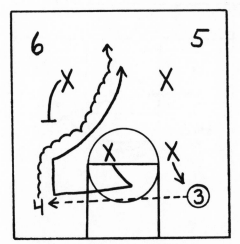

Diag. 140   Crosscourt Pass And Dribble Downcourt Against Press

OTHER FULL-COURT PRESSES

The 1–2–1–2, 1–3–2, and 3–1–2 full-court presses have a built-in feature that can make them superior to the 2–2 –2 press. They offer the defense the opportunity to challenge the inbounds pass by matching up, even when the matchups cease when the ball is put into play. The 1–2–1 and 1–3 have a player guarding the passer, always a difficult proposition, but the 3–1 can be even more difficult, when the "1" double-teams the best ballhandler while the other guards matchup.

The same 1–3–2 offensive alignment previously discussed can be used against these zone presses. An offensive variation sometimes used against zones is to rotate the wings, with the pivot either standing still, setting a screen for one of the wings, or breaking toward the baseline or midcourt. (Diagram 141).

Every team needs at least one dependable ballhandler capable of bringing the ball downcourt in one-on-one situations. If the ballhandler is highly skilled, she can beat the press and facilitate the fast break not only by forcing the one-on-one confrontation, but also by encouraging the guards to double-team her.

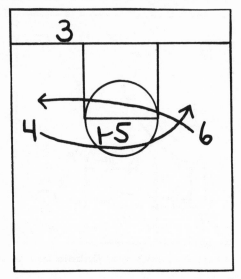

Diag. 141 Wing Rotation Against Zone Presses

FORCING THE DOUBLE-TEAM

Double-teaming can be one of the most potent of all defensive maneuvers. Merely the threat of it, such as the movement of an offside guard faking toward the dribbler, can panic some players into catching the ball or making a wild pass rather than assume the awesome responsibility of advancing the ball against two guards. Even experienced ballhandlers sometimes panic in the face of unexpected, well-organized double-teams.

A good ballhandler will attempt to force the defense to double-team, knowing that much of the effective strength of trapping lies in the *fear* element of encountering two or more guards unexpectedly. When alertness and aggressive attitude overrule a ballhandler's fear, double-teams lose their element of surprise, and the dribbler is free to attack the defense.

Much of any winning basketball team's success can be attributed to its ability to attack the opposition rather than waiting passively for the other team to strike. In most cases, victory goes to the team and players who control the action, or flow, of the game. Attackers control, while defenders merely react to the movements of those who attack.

The ballhandler who knowingly dribbles into a defensive double-team must know where to look for her teammates, and she must be able to identify the defensive changes brought about by her movements. She has to protect the ball while looking for open teammates, and she must then make the pass through, under, or over the guards to whatever teammate is open.

If she does all this, she has practically ensured the success of her team's fast break, at least as far as the outlet pass and favorable positioning of defensive personnel are concerned.

Against a 1–2–1–2 defense, for example, with the ball inbounded to the middle and passer O4 breaking to the opposite corner, O3 drives around X1, then slows down slightly, controlling the ball as she challenges X2. If X2 backs up, she continues to dribble toward half-court, prepared to pass to O5 whenever X2 accepts the challenge. (Diagram 142)

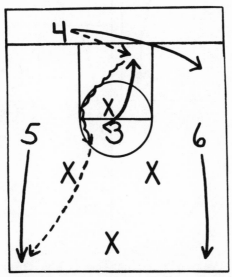

Diag. 142   A Good Ballhandler Attacking A Full-Court Press

A method of achieving the same result against a 3–1–2 press is to pass to O3 in the corner, with O4 breaking down the middle or to the side as O3 challenges X1 and X2. The pattern can be varied by lining up O3 and O5 at the midcourt corners, only *if* inbounder O6 is capable of making the long pass in the event that O4 is double-teamed *before* the bringin. (Diagrams 143–144)

Diag. 143   Fast-Breaking Against A 3–1–2 Zone Press

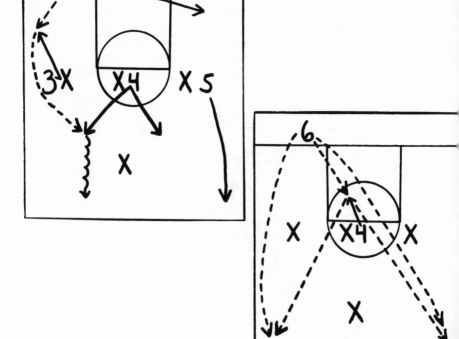

Diag. 144   Passing Patterns For 1–1–2 Offensive Setup Against 3–1–2 Zone Press

Half-Court Presses

The half-court presses are the most underrated aspect of girls' and women's basketball. Many teams deploy half-court presses, but few use them to their full potential the reasoning is perhaps, that the full-court presses are more likely to be effective in terms of forcing ten-second turnovers. Additionally, the half-court presses allow the offense to prepare its attack more carefully than full-court presses.

Half-court alignments however, put no less than four, and sometimes as many as six guards into a reasonably small area of the court. In a 3–2–1 half-court alignment, for example, *five* defensive players may be set within fifteen feet of half-court, and in such an alignment they drastically cut down the size of the dribbling and passing lanes. This affords the defense more opportunities to stop the dribbler, double-team, or cover the cutters without weakening their position. The offensive team nears half-court more quickly, but getting the ball past five defenders in a limited court area can be another matter altogether.

In other words, the full-court presses are more closely aligned with violations concerning the ten-second rule, while half-court presses are more likely to produce intercepted passes and held balls resulting from unexpected double-teaming.

The half-court presses seen most often are the 3–1–2 and 1–3–2. Others include the 3–2–1, 2–2–2, 1–2–1–2, and 1–2–2–1.

Approaches to beating the half-court presses generally are similar to those used in attacking full-court presses. A team can either set up to split the zone (Diagram 145), match up player-to-player in order to force one-on-one coverage, or match up and then split the zone by forcing the guards to double-team.

The first and possibly most important consideration in attacking half-court presses is the importance of the stationary forwards as scoring threats via the long pass. If the defense can eliminate the stationary forwards, even one of them, as an offensive threat they will have gained an extra advantage in an area of the court where they already had an advantage. This can be successful without weakening their defensive position. Therefore, in most half-court press offenses the stationary

Diag. 145 Forcing Openings In The 1–3–2 Half-Court Press

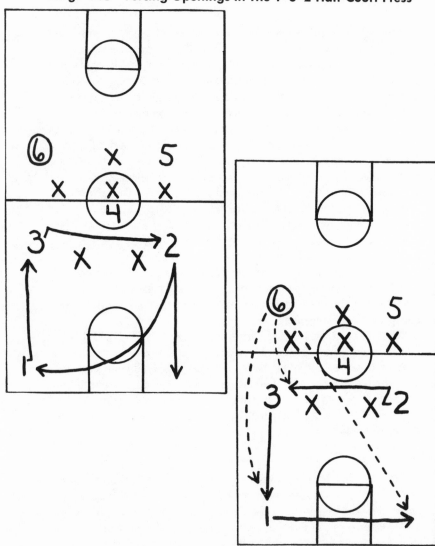

Diag. 146 Setting Up The Long Pass Against A Half-Court Press

forwards line up or break deep to the corners of the forecourt. Either method is acceptable, but in most cases, and against most defenses, they also serve those who only stand and wait in the corners.

Splitting can also be accomplished by matching up, especially from a 3–1–2 offensive formation. The ball is advanced up the middle of the court until the dribbler (O6 in Diagram 147), is challenged, in which case she passes to O5. O3 breaks to the sideline beyond half-court, and O6 breaks into the opening between X1, X2, and X3. O4 acts as a safety valve, in case O5 is unable to advance the ball by passing or dribbling. (Diagram 147)

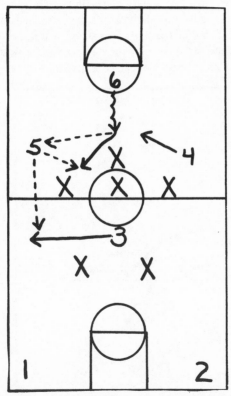

Diag. 147   Splitting The 1–3–2 Half-Court Press

One point must be made, however. The forwards must be alert not only to the movements of the defense, but also to their teammates' movements, as the team may find itself with five players on the offensive end of the court.

The keys to beating any press, lie in the forwards' calmness and alertness. Panic is the greatest foe of a team trying to get the ball across half-court against any kind of press. It is not easy to dribble calmly into two guards, or to wait patiently for a teammate to break free when unexpected trapping occurs, but the reward is often a layup for a forward at the other end of the court.

Calmness is only possible, then, when players are alert. The ballhandler must be alert to the approximate court position of all the other players, but even more importantly, the ballhandler's teammates must be alert to the movements of the defense in order to find the openings in the zone as it shifts. That such a skill is advanced, and found only in better players, is evident, but it is a necessary aspect of the task of beating the presses. Other half-court presses can be seen in the following Diagrams.

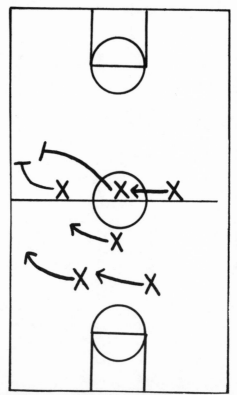

Diag. 148 3-1-2 Half-Court Pressing Movements

Diag. 149 1–3–2 Half-Court Pressing Movements

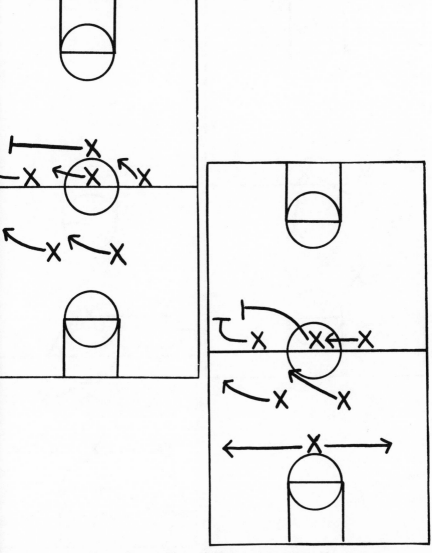

Diag. 150 3–2–1 Half-Court Pressing Movements

Diag. 151 2–2–2 Half-Court Pressing Movements

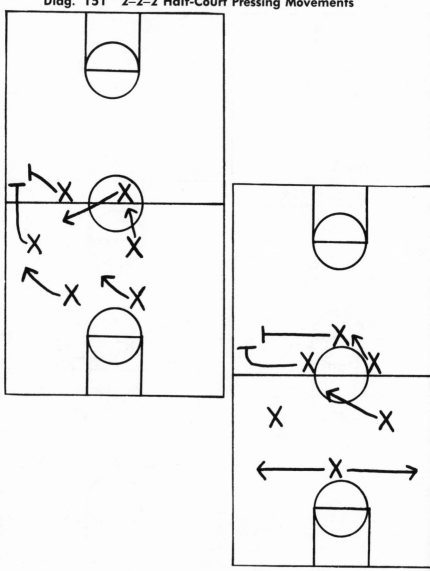

Diag. 152 1–2–2–1 Half-Court Pressing Movements

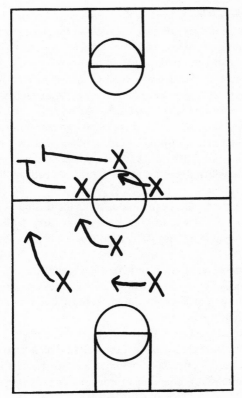

Diag. 153   1–2–1–2 Half-Court Pressing Movements

THE FAST BREAK

Organizing The Fast Break

Against all but the very weakest of defenses, the success or failure of a fast break is decided in the first three seconds after a team gains possession of the ball. By then, the rovers should have reacted to the changeover and begun dropping back to form the defense, and every hesitation by the forwards in advancing the ball downcourt during this lag decreases their chances of catching the defense offguard.

Reflecting the validity of this contention, many coaches teach their players that *the fast break starts while a team is on defense*. A team cannot fast break when it does not have the ball, so the players must be intent upon playing aggressively while on defense. Aggressive defense can force many sudden turnovers, each of which is a potential fast break.

In fact, despite the sudden quickness of fast break opportunities, team speed ranks no better than third behind anticipation and fast reaction in contributing to the creation of fast breaks. Additionally, speed for speed's sake is of little value. *Controlled* speed is a greater priority, because a fast-breaking team tends to make more ballhandling errors than a team deploying a controlled offense. As the tempo of the game increases, so do the chances of ballhandling mistakes. High-speed ballhandling is always a risky proposition.

Still, the team that has been thoroughly indoctrinated in a philosophy of fast-breaking will try to fast break every time they get their hands on the ball, believing that every possession is a fast break until the defense stops it.

Some of the advantages of fast-breaking include:

1. It provides an excellent way of beating presses, especially those that attempt to trap or double-team the ballhandler. It can also serve to bring teams out of their presses.

2. Fast breaking is essentially an offensive strategy that maintains steady pressure on the defense. A team that has been "burned" by fast breaks several times often becomes overcautious in its ballhandling, or cuts back its offensive rebounding in order to drop players back to stop the fast break.

3. Layups are the easiest shots in basketball, and the fast break increases the likelihood of a team's shooting layups.

4. It is an easy way to score points quickly. It can break up a close game, or aid a team in catching up when it gets behind.

5. It is exciting for the spectators and fun for the players, who often derive a great sense of accomplishment from participating in fast breaks.

There are no disadvantages per se in fast-breaking, but there are situations in which fast-breaking is unlikely to increase a team's chances of winning. Some of these situations include:

1. Teams with inept ballhandling will be unable to perform high-speed ballhandling maneuvers without losing the ball often, and turnovers off the fast break may yield fast breaks for the opponent.

2. When the opponents' fast break is clearly superior, a team's best chances often lie in slowing down the tempo of the game. Running teams win running games.

3. When a team's best ballhandler is in foul trouble, that team should either alter its fast break pattern to have someone else handle the ball, or abandon the fast break altogether. Because of the increased tempo of play, charging fouls are always a dangerous possibility in fast breaking.

Starting the Fast Break

The fast break can be started in any of three ways: from a turnover, a baseline bringin after the opponents score, or a defensive rebound.

Concerning turnovers, the advantages lie with the team that is fast breaking, especially when the ball remains in play, as in stealing the ball, intercepting passes, etc. In such cases, the dribbler's, or intended receiver's, momentum is usually toward her own basket, and when the turnover occurs, the offense should have no problem gaining a 3-on-2 or 2-on-1 player advantage. A team's highest percentage of successful fast breaks usually comes from turnovers.

Baseline bringins are not generally considered to be vehicles for fast breaking, but they can be, in situations like those contained in the previous section of this chapter, Beating The Presses. Scoring opportunities from fast breaks off presses are relatively infrequent, but they should not be overlooked.

The majority of fast break opportunities arise as a result of moving the ball downcourt quickly after getting a defensive rebound. The rebounder's first movement, after catching the ball in the air and protecting it as she comes down, should be to turn her body toward the nearer sideline and look downcourt for teammates breaking. Her head and eyes must be up, and she must look for teammates breaking, or the possibility of the fast break will be greatly reduced or eliminated.

An inexperienced ballhandler is likely to be more concerned with protecting the ball than looking for cutters, so it is very important to drill the defensive rebounders in their movements after gaining possession of the ball. The fast break will still succeed in some cases if the rebounder clears to the sideline with two or three quick dribbles before making the outlet pass, as long as she concentrates on getting the ball downcourt as quickly as possible.

Whether the rebounder dribbles downcourt or makes the outlet pass depends upon her ability to execute the fundamentals involved. If she chooses the former she should dribble as nearly as possible down the middle of the court. A straight line is the shortest distance between two points, and every unnecessary dribble toward the sidelines allows the defense more time to retreat and set up. She should advance the ball until she is challenged and/or stopped by the defense, at which time she relinquishes control of the fast break to a teammate. (Diagram 154)

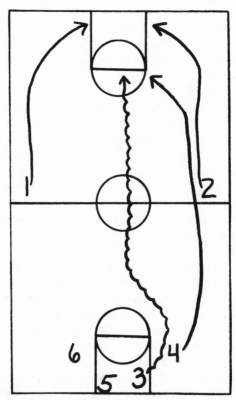

Diag. 154 Fast-Breaking With The Rebounder Taking The Ball Down The Middle

If the rebounder makes the outlet pass, it should be either a baseball pass or a two-hand overhead pass. The type of pass used depends on the individual, within the framework of certain guidelines.

The two-hand overhead pass is generally used for short passes, especially to the sideline. Since the hands are overhead in rebounding anyway, there is no wasted motion involved. The overhead is a quicker pass than the baseball pass, and it is more difficult to block because it is usually thrown as a lob pass rather than a line drive.

While time-consuming, the baseball pass is a more natural movement than the two-hand overhead pass. It can be thrown harder and for longer distances than the two-hand overhead, and it can be thrown as a lob pass or a line drive.

Moving the Ball Downcourt

The routes of the intended receivers of the outlet pass vary with the personnel and the number of passes the team expects to make in getting the ball downcourt. The rebounder, however, usually looks for her teammates breaking toward the sideline or toward the top of the circle at that end of the court.

If a team has one good ballhandler, and she is also the team's leading defensive rebounder, the coach might prefer that she forego the outlet pass in favor of dribbling downcourt herself, in effect, sacrificing some of the *speed* of the break for greater ball control.

If a team has one good ballhandler who does not get many rebounds, she can receive the outlet pass at the sideline or top of the circle to lead the fast break. (Diagram 155)

If a team has more than one good ballhandler in addition to the rebounders, they can have an outstanding fast break by sending their primary receiver to the top of the circle and their secondary receiver to the sideline after the rebound is claimed. This will give them two chances to complete the outlet pass instead of one.

The primary considerations involved in moving the ball downcourt at the greatest possible controlled speed are that the ball should be taken to the middle of the court as quickly as possible, and that the best dribbler should handle the ball as much as possible during the middle of the break. Even if she is stopped and has to pass off to a teammate, she can still fill the trailer's passing lane without dropping out of the fast break.

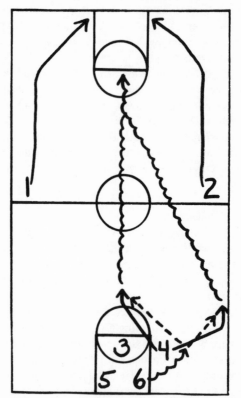

Diag. 155   One-Pass Fast Break Passing Routes

The Dribbler Leading The Fast Break

When the rebounder takes the ball downcourt, she attempts to move toward the center of the court, while her teammates fill the passing lanes along either sideline. The fourth forward should stay back as a safety valve in case the dribbler gets in trouble. The stationary forwards, originally lined up near half-court, fill the sideline passing lanes and advance toward the basket when the dribbler nears midcourt. Ideally, the wings at the defensive end of the court wait at half-court, and one of them becomes the trailer.

THE ONE-PASS FAST BREAK

Although many teams' best ballhandlers are also their best rebounders, fast breaks are usually slower when the rebounder leads the fast break, as opposed to passing to a teammate to start the break. A quick, sure outlet pass yields a quicker start for the fast break than does dribbling in almost all cases, regardless of whether the pass is to the sideline or the top of the circle. The offense's primary goal in fast breaking is to get the ball downcourt as quickly as possible, and the outlet pass can accomplish this objective in less time than the fastest dribbler.

When a player breaks to the sideline to receive the outlet pass, she should already be breaking downcourt when she receives the pass. She should not be breaking toward the sideline when she catches the ball because she will have to make a ninety degree turn before advancing the ball downcourt. In a one-pass fast break, she will dribble toward the middle and advance the ball until stopped by the defense.

When the intended ballhandler breaks to the top of the circle as in Diagram 155, it is often necessary for the rebounder to dribble two or three times to the side before passing the ball, in order to complete the outlet pass to the top of the circle. Taking the ball outside before making the outlet pass slows down the fast break slightly, but it is often necessary in order to pass the ball over the guards' reaching arms.

THE TWO-PASS FAST BREAK

The quickest way to get the ball downcourt on a fast break after a defensive rebound is to pass directly to a teammate breaking toward, or from, the top of the circle. Unfortunately, though, this pattern is rather easily defensed. If the opponents know that only one girl is breaking, they can send three girls after the rebound, with the fourth girl covering the outlet pass receiver. (Diagram 156)

On the other hand, when the defensive team can afford to have two girls filling the outlet passing lanes, the classic fast break pattern is established. In the two-pass fast break, the rebounder passes to the sideline to a breaking teammate, who passes to a teammate in the middle and continues across half court as the trailer. Ideally, the sideline cutter/trailer should be the team's *second best* ballhandler.

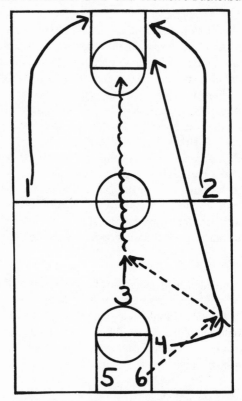

Diag. 156   The Two-Pass Fast Break

Both the sideline cutter, known as the trailing wing, and the forward in the middle, the point forward, must be alert to unexpected stops and sudden movements of the guards in order to avoid charging fouls.

The second phase of the fast break is completed when the ball crosses half-court. If the ballhandler reaches half-court without undue pressure, she is likely to achieve the 3–2 setup at her own end of the court.

Finishing the Fast Break
1. The Stationary Forwards—wings. They should be set up near half-court at either sideline while the opponents have the ball. When the

fast break begins, they must resist the temptation to rush wildly toward their basket. They should, instead, wait until the point forward nears halfcourt then move toward their baseline, staying near the sideline until they reach a point approximately even with the free throw line. Then they begin angling toward the basket. They should go all the way to the basket rather than stop outside the lane for a short jump shot, and in order to do this they should not be over four to five feet ahead of the point forward. If they get ahead of the dribbler, they should slow down, not stop.

The wings should never take off-balance or forced shots from the fast break. If the shooter is not clear for a layup or open jump shot, she should take the ball outside and wait for her teammates to set up in their regular offensive patterns. Forced shots can inspire the defense to greater efforts by convincing them that their efforts have succeeded in disrupting the fast break.

2. The Point Forward. The point forward's first concern is ball control, not speed. If she has crossed midcourt without already being seriously challenged by the defense, she should direct her attentions toward forcing the defense to guard her. If they fail to, she should be prepared to drive between them and shoot the layup, especially when the stationary guards are incorrectly aligned side-by-side instead of one-up, one-back. The greatest mistake the point forward can make is to stop her dribble outside, or beyond the foul line, without being challenged by the guards.

If a guard stops her before she reaches the free throw line, a quick pass to either wing will set up a two-on-one situation for the other forwards. Still, the defense knows this, and in most cases they will drop back to guard the three-on-two, an easier proposition than covering the two-on-one.

In the three-on-two pattern, the point forward must not venture inside the free throw line, with the single exception previously noted. She should stop between the top of the circle and the free throw line, and she should make a definite pause before passing or shooting. This momentary pause is necessary to freeze the guards' movements and force them to commit themselves to a certain line of defense. The ingredients of a successful fast break are, controlling the ball at the free throw line, forming the offensive triangle (three-on-two), and making no more passes than absolutely necessary at the end of the fast break.

The point forward should shoot from the free throw line every time the guards drop back to cover the wings. When either guard covers her, she must be skilled enough to watch both defenders' movements and pass to the wing on the unguarded side. Against all but the most skilled defenders, she can freeze the guards by stopping at the free throw line, pausing to fake the pass to one wing, and then passing to the opposite wing for the layup. (Diagram 157)

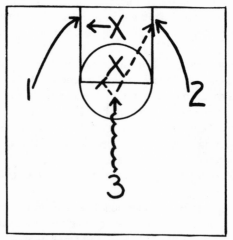

Diag. 157   3-on-2 Fast Break, Faking Left And Passing Right

Some coaches prefer that their point forwards veer toward a corner of the free throw line at the end of the fast break. Such a move might seem detrimental to the balance of the offensive triangle, but it can simplify the offensive task by drawing the outside guard out of position to drop back and cover the second pass. At the same time, this allows the point forward to use a bounce pass directly off the dribble to the wing with the ball never having been caught with both hands. (Diagram 158)

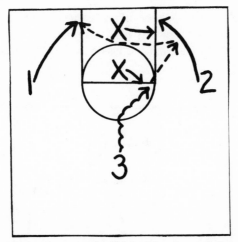

Diag. 158   Veering Right In The 3-on-2 Fast Break

The offense is not necessarily bogged down even when the defense can get three guards back to stop the fast break. The point forward veers to one side as before, but instead of passing to the wing, she passes across the free throw line to the trailer for the open shot. (Diagram 159)

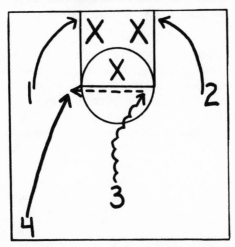

Diag. 159   4-on-3 Fast Break With Pass To Trailer

Even a three-on-three situation off the fast break can be exploited by an alert offense. The point forward passes to a wing, then veers opposite to screen for the other wing, who cuts inside for the return pass and layup. (Diagram 160)

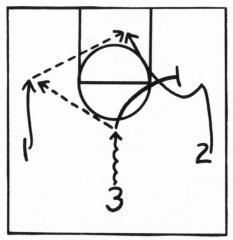

Diag. 160   3-on-3 Fast Break

To summarize, then, the point forward's alternatives include passing to either wing, taking the shot from the free throw line, faking and driving, or passing to the trailer.

The problem is to provide practice and repetition of the three-on-two pattern and its nuances to the extent that the point forward's actions and reactions are spontaneous and reflexive rather than predictable and stereotyped. Leading the fast break can be one of the most creative ventures in all of team sports, once the ballhandler's confidence and ability have reached a level where she can change her movements or passing options when the defense adjusts to one pattern.

Part II
TEAM DEFENSE

I am often put on a top player on the other team and I take pride in doing a (defensive) job on him. What kind of job can I do? I can force him out of his favorite spots on the court, take his best shots and passes away from him, and steal the ball from him a fair number of times. These won't show in the stats, but they're as important as points.

Jerry West,
Basketball My Way

5
Player-To-Player Defensive Team Techniques

The day is gone when a coach can merely note that the team used a player-to-player defense in scouting opponents, then go on to note other aspects of their game without further investigation of the defense. Due to refinements over the years within the basic structure of player-to-player defense, the information noted above is of no more value to a coach than his knowing that they played a zone defense. There are different kinds of player-to-player defensive team tactics, techniques, coverages, and strategies, and the success or failure of any given player-to-player offensive pattern will be determined at least partly by the type of player-to-player defense used.

Player-To-Player Defensive Coverages

STRAIGHT PLAYER-TO-PLAYER DEFENSE

Straight defense is basic defense. It is playing the defense as it was originally designed, without the frills or risks inherent in other kinds of defense. In short, it is the safest form of player-to-player defense, if, indeed, any form of player-to-player defense can be called *safe*.

In straight defense, each guard is responsible for defending a single forward, trying to stay with her wherever she goes, except when blocked out by screening or crossing movements.

By far the most difficult aspect of team player-to-player defense is that of combatting screens. In straight defense, the guard attempts to slide through or go behind the screener rather than switching, although switching may not be ruled out entirely. Playing straight involves the guard's doing all she can to stay with her forward in screening situations, but when she cannot, *she* calls the switch. In other forms of player-to-player defense, the switch is either automatic or called by the screening forward's guard.

A team inexperienced in switching techniques is better off playing straight defense than attempting to master other player-to-player variations.

SWITCHING PLAYER-TO-PLAYER DEFENSE

In the strictest switching defense, guards ordinarily do not attempt to slide through screens. Instead, they switch defensive responsibilities automatically whenever forwards cross, almost as if they were playing a zone defense. Switching defense provides excellent coverage against outside weave patterns.

If the guards are inexperienced, the switches should be called orally by the screener's guard, in order to ensure that both guards understand that they are supposed to switch. There is no discrepancy in calling the switches between straight and switching defenses. The principle is, whenever a guard attempts to go over the top of a screen, *she* will be in a better position to know whether she will make it or not, so *she* is responsible for calling the switch. Conversely, when the guards are playing a switching defense, the screening forward's guard is more likely to know when to effect the switch, so the responsibility for calling the switch is then hers.

The problem associated with verbal commands in notifying teammates of the intended transfer is that the same information is then made available to the opponents as well. If this is the case, the screening guard is likely to maintain her position rather than rolling to the basket, while the outside forward pivots and goes back around the screen.

When the guards are experienced and aggressive, they may choose to forego verbal signals in switching, preferring instead to make switching automatic and nonverbal. This, in effect, transforms their player-to-player coverage into a semi-zone defense. Automatic switches are risky and difficult, but if done quickly and aggressively, in most cases, they should be as effective as those used in straight defense.

Switching defense is least likely to work in situations where the forward receiving the screen is a good outside shot as well as a good dribbler. It is also dangerous when the switch creates a mismatch favoring the offense, such as when a tall foward defensed by a tall guard sets a screen for a teammate being defensed by a short guard. In the resulting switch, there is a very real danger of the inside pass. The tall guard then must not only make the switch, but stop the ballhandler from making the inside pass by guarding her closely and aggressively.

SINKING PLAYER-TO-PLAYER DEFENSE

Sinking, or sagging, defense consists of dropping off of outside forwards when they are not imminent scoring threats in order to increase defensive strength inside. Sinking is often advisable away from the ball, when a forward is a poor outside shooter, or in inside double-teaming situations.

As is the case with almost all types of player-to-player defense, the guard must be able to divide her concentration without weakening her defense. In Diagram 161, X3 might be required to keep up with her forward, the ball, and an inside forward simultaneously. Her priorities remain the same, however: (1) her forward, (2) the inside forward, and (3) the ball.

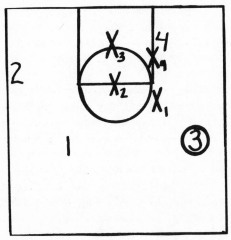

Diag. 161   Sinking Toward The Ball

The sinking defense is similar to zone defense and is, in fact, often mistaken for a matchup zone, especially when the offense features outside play rather than inside cutters. If a team employs a stationary post player without inside cutters, it is likely to have a great deal of trouble with sinking defenses.

Sinking will not work against effective outside shooting, intricate cutting and screening patterns, or double-post offenses. It should be most effective against outside patterns, teams with weak outside shooting, offenses with few cutters, single-post offenses, or stationary post players.

TRAPPING PLAYER-TO-PLAYER DEFENSE

Virtually the only skill in basketball more difficult and risky than defensive trapping is the forwards' ability to escape them with a minimal loss of self-respect and ball possession. A team that traps is likely to be an outstanding defensive team. This is due to the fact that the trapping movement must be extremely aggressive to keep the ball from escaping the trap and giving the offense a three-on-two advantage, or five-on-four in full-court situations.

Trapping within player-to-player defense may occur anywhere on the court, although certain situations are more conducive to double-teaming the ballhandler than others. Trapping can be extremely dangerous to the defense if used indiscriminately, so the guards usually choose their spots carefully. They prefer situations in which two or more forwards are in close proximity (e.g., crossing patterns, screening, splitting the post, weave patterns, etc.), or those situations where the ballhandler's dribbling and or passing lanes are drastically reduced, such as the offensive baseline.

Although they are similar, *double-teaming* is not synonymous with trapping. Whereas double-teaming may or may not be premeditated on the guard's part, trapping is always a planned, aggressive attempt by two or more forwards simultaneously to force the ballhandler to relinquish control of the ball. The defense tries to force their opposition into faulty passing or continuing to dribble in a situation where dribbling is clearly contraindicated. Also, double-teaming does not necessarily refer to defensing the ballhandler, as noted by the *sinking* defense that often involves double-teaming, for instance. Trapping, however, seldom involves double-guarding anyone besides the dribbler.

The objective of trapping may be either to stop the dribbler in a court position from which she will have trouble passing to a teammate, or to steal the ball. In the former, the dribbler is allowed to dribble to the baseline, for example, where her guard assumes an overguarding position to stop her forward progress. A second guard then leaves her forward to stop her from dribbling out of the corner or passing the ball away. Except with outstanding defensive personnel, this maneuver is more likely to be successful from a zone situation rather than from a player-to-player defense.

Trapping outside forwards is somewhat easier, requiring only quick, aggressive guards with a sense of anticipation and timing, to take advantage of forwards' ballhandling weaknesses. In Diagram 162, for example, the guards' initial movements and reactions to the screen appear to be a simple defensive switch, except when the guard continues to advance low towards the ball instead of assuming a straight-on position between the dribbler and the basket. Her purpose is not to steal the ball, but to turn the dribbler into her teammate, who is moving toward the ball from the dribbler's blind side, ignoring the screening forward's roll.

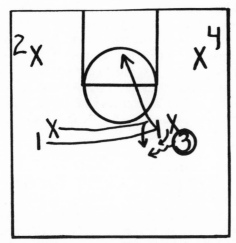

Diag. 162   Defensive Trapping Off A Screen-and-Roll

When the guards are successful, they will have the ball and a good fast break opportunity. If they fail to get the ball, they still might be able to stop the inside pass and force a held ball situation. If they are not successful in stopping the ballhandler from passing the ball, they must rely on their teammates' anticipating and covering the most dangerous passing zones until they can drop back to regroup defensively.

The trapping player-to-player defense will not work with inexperienced, mediocre, or passive guards, nor is it likely to be successful against good ballhandlers, clearouts, or continuity offenses featuring screens and movement away from the ball.

PRESSING PLAYER-TO-PLAYER DEFENSE

Pressing, or pressure defense refers to guarding offensive players closely at all times, whether or not they have the ball. It requires that all four defenders be fundamentally sound, well-conditioned, and extremely alert. Pressing guards harass their fowards when they have the ball, fighting through screens, blocks, and crossing patterns whenever possible. They also try to keep them from getting the ball when they do not have it. Their objective is to maintain constant defensive pressure on the offense, forcing the forwards out of their regular offensive patterns into one-on-one situations.

Pressing defense is most effective against offenses characterized by indecisive ballhandling, little offensive movement or screening situations, and outside shooting. It is often seen in the waning moments of a game when a team is behind and needs the ball, and individually is used occasionally to try to keep the ball away from an outstanding forward. Against overall weak ballhandling, it is the most potent defense a team can use.

COMBINATION PLAYER-TO-PLAYER DEFENSE

Bearing in mind the guards' individual abilities and skills, as well as the teams's defensive objectives, it is possible to combine certain variations of the basic player-to-player defense to produce refined editions superior to their components. For instance, trapping defense is usually played as straight defense, except when circumstances favor trapping movements. It can also be combined, however, with either switching (trap sometimes, switch sometimes), or pressing defense.

Sinking and pressing defense are especially compatible within a single defense. The forward with the ball receives pressure, except when she is a poor shooter, while other guards sink off their forwards to defend against inside passes.

Other successful combinations may occur to the coach (including the same tactics and combinations from zone alignments), as long as the guards understand their duties and responsibilities within whatever systems they are using.

Defensing Continuity Patterns

A continuity offense is a sequence of set plays allowing repetition of an offensive pattern without the forwards' having to reset themselves in their original positions. Continuity patterns possess no intrinsic advantages of set plays except continuous movement and the fact that the constant repetition of the basic pattern tends to lull the guards into relaxing their vigilance as they move.

There are two basic types of continuity offenses, outside patterns (e.g., the three or four-player weaves), and inside patterns (the shuffle and wheel offenses.)

Much of the strength of the outside patterns can be neutralized by the sinking defenses, particularly when the offense has three forwards outside and a fourth forward at the high post. In defensing the weaves, guards should synchronize their movements so that the ballhandler's guard never has to move behind a teammate in guarding the dribbler. The guards whose forwards do *not* have the ball, in other words, should step backward to allow the dribbler's guard to pass.

Trapping can also be used effectively against weave patterns, but switching defenses should be avoided. Against good offensive teams, the guards will never be able to keep up with the switches and guard the high post too.

The most common defense against inside patterns is a combination of sinking defense and switching. Since both the shuffle and wheel movements involve screening away from the ball, switching facilitates the guards' defensive positioning, while sinking gives them more time to pick up their switches.

Trapping and pressure defense seldom work against inside patterns, since trapping requires forwards near the ball, and continuity offenses were designed to work against pressing defenses.

A risky but effective defensive maneuver is to stop the outlet pass or the pass that initiates the forwards' movements. For example, when the defense knows that an offensive pattern always begins with a certain forward passing to a teammate breaking outside, they can sometimes disrupt the entire offense by stopping the initial pass. Of course, the guard must be alert to the possibility of her forward's faking the outside move, then breaking to the basket in a backdoor move.

When the initial pass is made, inside screening patterns can be made more difficult by the ballhandler's guard doing everything she can to disturb her concentration and vision.

Defensive Automatics

An *automatic* is a spontaneous offensive or defensive movement designed to counteract the movement of the opponent. Among the more familiar offensive automatics are backdoor cuts, clearouts, and dribbling reverses.

Since automatics are primarily responsive in nature, defensive automatics take the form of general principles and procedures:

1. The offense normally resorts to using automatics only when their regular patterns have been stopped. Guards should, therefore, play an offense "straight" until they have determined what the forwards are trying to do.

2. The defense's first priority is *always* to stop the layup. If the ballhandler or cutter is in position to move to the basket for a shot, the guard should concentrate on stopping the layup. If the forward pulls up for a short jumper or hook shot, at least the guard is able to avert the layup.

3. Switches are never automatic, except when a team is playing a strict switching defense, and when a forward has broken free from her guard. In all other cases, switches should be called orally.

4. Every guard bears the responsibility for warning her teammates when screens or picks are being set. Whether her opponents hear her warnings or not, should not affect her actions; after all, the opponents know what they are going to do anyway, so they will not be learning anything from what they hear.

5. Sometimes forwards use double screens with two-way cutting lanes to break a teammate into the clear. When this occurs, the guards must make sure that the second and third cutters are covered. Defense does not stop just because one cutter has gone around a screen!

Defensing The Double Screen

The basic double-screening situation involves a ballhandler, two forwards setting the double screen, and sometimes a cutter. In the first case, where an outside forward with the ball has two teammates screening for her simultaneously, the dribbler will go around the screen in whatever direction she thinks will yield her the best shot. If the guards switch, she will pass to one of the screening forwards rolling to the basket. The guards should defense it as a simple give-and-go, calling the switch as soon as possible, then attempting to stop the drive and inside pass. If they stop those two movements, they will likely have foiled the entire double-screen, since no cutters are left to continue the movement.

In the second case, where a cutter has a double screen away from the ball, more vigilance is required of all four guards. As was shown in Diagrams 65–69, O2 protects the ball while dribbling, as O1 and O3 move to set a double screen for O4 opposite the ball. O4, having the option of going either way around the screen, will go whichever way she thinks the guards will have the most trouble defending. If she goes in front of the screen, X1 should pick her up, while X4 moves to guard O1. X1 will stay with O4 as she clears the lane, attempting to keep her from receiving the pass. If O4 goes *behind* the screen, X3 should pick her up, with X4 moving to guard O3.

After O4 clears, either O3 or O1 will be the next cutter, but whoever it is, she may move around the screen before cutting, necessitating another defensive switch.

Finally, whatever forward is left may cut without the benefit of a screen as her direction depends largely upon the position of whichever guard is left defending her. Her break most often occurs away from the basket, toward the corner of the free throw lane.

Situational Defense

DEFENSING BRINGINS

The intensity of how a team defenses backcourt sideline bringins is largely determined by the guards' defensive skills and the coach's preferences. The three basic strategies are to: 1. employ pressing defense to make the forwards work to get the ball inbounds, 2. defend the inbounds pass, then drop back into a half-court press when the ball is inbounded successfully, and 3. send the rovers downcourt to set up at the defensive end without pressing the inbounds pass.

Regardless of the team's defensive strategy or skills, or where the ball is inbounded, the stationary forwards should be expected to play defense while the opponents have the ball at their end of the court.

In regard to pressing at the sideline, one guard should be assigned the task of defensing the inbounds passer, and she should never turn her back on the passer. Because that forward cannot dribble past her or go anywhere until she has passed the ball, the guard is free to jump, wave her arms in the air, or perform other distractions without fear of getting beaten, as long as she can stay with her forward after the pass is made. A favorite way of starting the fast break from the backcourt sideline is for the forward, who is receiving the pass, to return it quickly to the inbounding forward breaking downcourt.

A risky defensive maneuver that sometimes is effective in special situations is the double-teaming of the opponents' best ballhandler and single-guarding of the other forwards, while neglecting the inbounds passer. Such a move will sometimes surprise the forwards into turnovers like failing to get the ball into play within five seconds, but, because of the danger of the return pass to the inbounder breaking downcourt when the defense cannot contain the forwards, the guards must choose their situations carefully. The most favorable situation is one where the opponents rely heavily upon one forward for most of their ballhandling, although circumstances sometimes require its use in *unfavorable* circumstances, such as the latter part of a game when the defense needs to regain possession without unduly risking fouls.

The only effective pressing defense against sideline bringins in player-to-player defense. Although zone presses present more obstacles to the forwards in getting the ball downcourt, they are ineffectual in stopping the inbounds pass. In other words, where backcourt bringins are concerned, if you want to stop the entire offense, us a zone, and if you want to stop a single player, pass, or movement, use a player-to-player defense.

Defensing the sidelines bringin plays is basic, with three notable points worthy of consideration:

1. Forwards should never be allowed to catch an inbounds pass while heading toward their own basket. The guards should overguard their forwards in such a manner that, if they are to free themselves to receive the pass, they will have to break away from their own basket.

2. In pressing to stop the inbounds pass, the guards will not always be able to keep up with their forwards and watch the pass too. Since inexperienced or unskilled forwards tend to watch the ball as it moves through the air toward them (sometimes even lifting their arms in preparing to receive the pass), a guard who knows her forward's ability can sometimes steal or block such passes by watching her forward's eyes and/or hand movements and positioning her hands and arms accordingly. This technique will not work against smart, experienced forwards. They will either fake as above, then break somewhere else when the guard commits herself, or conceal the ball's movement until it is too late for the guard to stop it. It should succeed, however, against most opponents in most sideline bringin situations.

3. The stationary guards should do their best to discourage long passes from the backcourt sideline to the forwards at their end. The only real chance of fast breaking directly from the backcourt sideline bringin is the long pass that would create one-on-one or two-on-two matchups inside, so the stationary guards should take necessary measures to prevent such passes.

Another type of sideline backcourt defensive strategies is to attempt to stop the inbounds pass, then drop back into a half-court press. A team may also drop back to set up at the defensive end, relying on the stationary forwards to supply a measure of defense. The only situations when a team is justified in dropping back without pressing are when the opponents' fast break is imminent, or when the guards are extremely slow, unskilled, or in foul trouble.

Forecourt sideline defensive patterns are similar to those employed in the backcourt, except that less emphasis is placed on overguarding because defensive mistakes in the forecourt usually yield two-on-one advantage for the offense. Therefore, forwards should not be over-guarded closely outside unless the guard can maintain defensive control without giving up the backdoor movement or lob pass inside over her head.

The first priority in defensing offensive baseline bringins is that, without exception, a guard must be assigned to defense the inbounds passer. If the defense neglects this apparently meaningless consideration—to double-team a superior forward, for example—they open themselves to the possibility of the inbounder bouncing the ball off a guard's back, catching it, and scoring from under the basket. The ball is in play as soon as it touches any player in bounds.

A second consideration for the defense is that, at least until the ball is inbounded, the guards should cover the forwards player-to-player. A zone defense will not work when applied to baseline bringin plays, although the team may drop back into a zone as soon as possible after the inbounds pass.

Third, guards should attempt to force their forwards to catch the inbounds pass *going away from the basket*. The only possible exception to this rule is when a guard does not want her forward to get the ball at all, and overplays her to stop the most obvious pass. Of course, the guard must be extremely confident of her abilities before attempting such a maneuver.

Finally, whenever possible, guards defending inside forwards should position themselves to watch both their forward and the inbounds passer, in order to be ready for the lob pass over their heads. If unable to watch both, the guard should watch her forward, guarding her closely and waving her arms overhead to deflect passes when she expects or anticipates a lob pass over her head. Although an experienced forward will not give away the pass by looking for it until it is beyond the guard, *most* forwards will watch the flight of the ball from the time it leaves the passer's hand, and the guard can judge the proximity and angle of the ball in flight by watching the forward's eyes.

DEFENSING FREE THROWS

From a defensive standpoint, there are four aspects of situations involving missed free throws that should be taken into account in preparing for, and dealing with, the opponents.

First, steps should be taken to prevent the opponents from claiming the rebound. When the opponents are shooting, the two best rebounding guards should occupy the inside positions on either side of the lane, and a third guard should line up in the third position to block out the shooter. The inside guards block out the forwards in the second positions by stepping diagonally into the lane to a position between the forwards and the basket. The farther away from the basket a guard is able to establish rebounding positioning, the less likely her forward will be able to gain the rebound without fouling her.

Positioning is vital to rebounding efficacy. A girl can become an effective rebounder with average jumping ability if she asserts herself aggressively in blocking out and going after the ball. The inside guards should not step toward the basket until they have already established rebounding position on the forwards in the second position. In other words, they must strive to keep the forwards from going to the basket or acquiring positioning equality.

A second factor in defensing opponents' free throws is, if the two inside guards block out their forwards and a third guard moves in front of the shooter, the rebounding advantage can go to the fourth guard, lined up in third position. (Diagram 163)

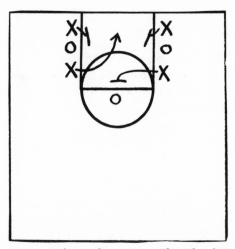

Diag. 163 Rebounding From The Third Position

The two inside guards should step across the forwards' path in such a manner as to deny access to the middle of the lane. At this point the forwards' choices are either to jump over the inside guards, or attempt to go around them to the outside. If they choose the former, they risk fouling, and if they choose the latter, the fourth guard should have a direct path to the rebound in the center of the lane.

A variation of this pattern is for the rebounding guard in the third position to line up on the side of the lane next to the opponents' best rebounder, helping the inside guard to keep that forward from getting the rebound.

The strategy outlined above underscores the contention that a player can contribute to her team's rebounding efforts even when she gathers few rebounds herself, as long as she denies them to the forward she is blocking out.

A third factor contributing to achieving and maintaining defensive rebounding superiority is the threat of the fast break off defensive rebounds. The opponents are hardly likely to send all four forwards after the rebound if they know that their opponents will fast break whenever they get the rebound. If a team fast breaks successfully off defensive rebounds, the opponents' forwards will tend to drop back to stop the break, thus further weakening their offensive rebounding strength.

The positioning for fast breaking off the rebound are many and varied, although the actions of the inside guards and the guard blocking out the shooter are the same as before until they get the ball. A way of initiating the fast break without tipping it off is for the fourth guard to line up in the third position as shown in Diagram 164, and, then, break outside to the sideline or to the top of the circle to receive the outlet pass when an inside guard claims the rebound.

The fourth aspect of defensing missed free throws is that of stopping the opponents' fast break when they obtain defensive rebounds.

The forward in the second position can sometimes get position by faking a move to the inside, then moving toward the baseline before the guard can counter her movement.

When a forward has absolutely no chance of recovering the rebound she can still stop the fast break if she can tap the ball back toward the basket, out of bounds, or to a teammate stationed on that side. Before attempting the latter, however, she should know whether the teammate is covered by the fourth guard.

Diag. 164 Outlet Passing Routes In Fast Breaking Off Defensive Rebounds

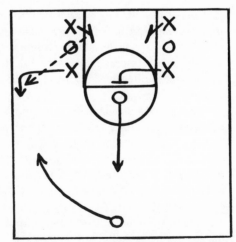

Diag. 165 Defensing An Offensive Free Throw

If an inside guard gets the rebound, the forward on that side should apply immediate defensive pressure to stop her from dribbling downcourt, and to hinder the outlet pass.

The fourth forward may be stationed behind a forward in the second position, or she may set up outside to slow down the fast break, depending upon individual preferences and ability, the game situation, and the strength of the opponents' fast break. Also, if the opponents use only three lane positions, setting the fourth guard at the sideline or elsewhere to hasten the formation of their fast break, the fourth forward may elect to cover the outlet pass by defensing her player-to-player until teammates can drop back to help stop the break.

COMBATTING THE STALLS

Two previously discussed tactics, pressure defense and trapping, are likely to provide the best defense against stalling. Pressing will not only keep pressure on the ballhandler, but if the other guards are able to apply similar pressure to *their* forwards, the dribbler, unable to pass off to a teammate, will be forced to take a hasty, low-percentage shot or risk a possession violation.

Such strategy is not easy, of course. The forwards are seldom so obliging as to stand idly by watching the dribble. Also the guards away from the ball, risk backdoor movements and layups, if in their zealous overguarding to stop the outside pass they forget to cover the inside route as well. If the pressure defense is to work effectively, however, they must cover as many offensive movements as they can with maximum pressure on their forwards.

Trapping is a standard defensive procedure in dealing with stalls, applied as judiciously or desperately as the situation dictates. Ideally, trapping should occur only when two forwards are close together, such as when a forward moves toward the ballhandler to receive a pass at close quarters, or in crossing patterns. In game situations, however, necessity often overrules prudence. When a team is behind in the latter stages of a game and will lose if the defense cannot regain possession of the ball, they may have to resort to trapping when the forwards are spread out to the corners of the half-court.

Of course, trapping against a spread offense is far less likely to be successful than when forwards cross, but the possible end, losing, tends to dictate the means. When a team must press and trap in such circumstances, their best bet is to keep the ball away from the best ballhandling forwards and trap the weaker ballhandlers.

If the best ballhandler has the ball, she will have to pass or shoot sooner or later, so her guard should play her straight until she passes the ball away, then guard her closely enough to discourage the dribbler from passing to her. The dribbler's guard can help out by overguarding in the direction of the opponents' best ballhandler when the dribbler picks up the ball.

When trapping a weak ballhandler in spread offense, the guard defending the opponents' best ballhandler should not be involved in the trapping. She should instead maintain tight enough defensive pressure on the forwards to keep the ball away from her. With one guard pressing the best ballhandler away from the ball and two other guards trapping the dribbler, the rest of the half court consists of two forwards and a single guard. Thus outnumbered, the lone guard must not commit herself to defensing either forward until the dribbler has definitely commited herself to passing to one of the forwards. If the trap occurs in the midcourt area, perhaps the best area for the fourth guard to be stationed is in the vicinity of the free throw line.

DEFENSING JUMP BALLS

While the objective of jump ball situations is usually to gain or maintain possession of the ball, there are times when a team should be more concerned with stopping the opponents from scoring or fast breaking than with controlling the tip. If a player is sure that she will lose the tip, she should alert her teammates by reminding them to defense it, and then check to see that they are positioned correctly before stepping into the jumping circle.

If the jumper is clearly outclassed, she might be able to get her opponent off balance by crowding in close to the edge of her half of the jumping circle, or she may jump early in an attempt to entice her opponent into jumping early and throwing off her timing and control of the ball as she tips it. The jumper must stay in her jumping semicircle until she or her opponent touch the ball.

Players other than the jumper carry most of the responsibility for stopping the opponents' fast break, or at least slowing them down. When the opponents use verbal signals to key the direction of the tip, the guards sometimes can pick up the keys and use the information to their own advantage. For example, many teams use the "clock" method, likening the jumping circle to a giant clock face, with the number called referring to the direction the ball will be tapped: *six* will be directly behind the jumper, *three* will be to her right, *twelve* directly in front of her, etc.

The players outside the circle are not allowed to move after the referee "sets" them, or warns them to keep their positions, until the ball is touched by either player after the toss. They should assume a solid defensive stance with feet and elbows wide and hands high, and if they anticipate their teammate's losing the tip, they should be in a position to get back on defense quickly. If they have been able to translate the opponents' cues, they may double-team the receiver or attempt to steal the tip by stepping in front of the intended receiver.

If the opponents have no called plays, they may be keying the tip to the open areas of the court, and in that case, the guards have no choice but to set up defensively and hope for the best. They should not try to steal the tip with no advance information to guide their movements. A good rule of thumb is, never surrender a possible advantage needlessly, but always concede the opponents' obvious initial advantages by dropping back to a position where those advantages are least likely to result in their scoring.

CENTER CIRCLE JUMP BALLS

Applying the principle that the straight line is the shortest distance between two points, the most expedient possible fast break occurs when the tip is directed to a forward at twelve o'clock. Therefore, the defense must first cover this possibility before dealing with other problems.

The distinguishing feature of defensive center jump alignments is that there are always four guards in the defensive half-court. If the outcome of the tip is uncertain, or if the opponents do not fast break often, the team may drop back only one guard as a precaution against a fast break. If there is no doubt that the opponents will win the tip, however, two guards may be dropped back.

Although it is important to avoid surrendering layups off the fast break, especially at the beginning or end of the game, the guards have some leeway in anticipating the direction of the tip and attempting to double-team or intercept the ball.

This is especially true since they always have two stationary guards back to slow down the break until help arrives.

The guards must be alert to the possibility of the opponents' setting screens to free teammates for the break. Unless they are outstanding defensive players, the guards should drop back and set up as quickly as possible, rather than trying to press the forward who received the tip.

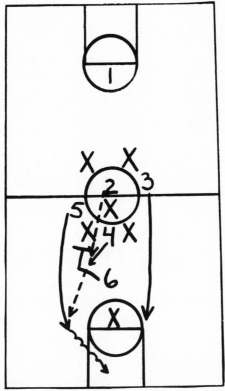

Diag. 166   Quick Opener Against Semi-Defensive Jump Ball Alignment

BACKCOURT JUMP BALL SITUATIONS

The easiest way to determine a team's best defensive strategy at any given moment in a game is to reverse the situation and determine what the forwards would most like to see happen, and then plan the defense accordingly. In the present situation, defensing a jump ball at the opponents' end of the court, their first preference would be tapping the ball toward their own basket to a teammate for a two to four foot shot.

Therefore, the defense's first priority at that end of the court should be to eliminate the inside shot or layup, which can be accomplished by either of two alignments, as shown in Diagrams 167-168.

Diag. 167 Defensing The Tip At The Backcourt Circle

Diag. 168 Variation Of Defensive Alignment At Backcourt Circle

Of the two, the former is clearly superior. Although neither alignment is likely to completely shut out the possibility of the clear shot off the tap, at least the former will only give up the outside shot, while the latter can yield a close shot for the offense (Diagram 169). Also the former automatically double-teams inside forwards every time the ball is tipped inside, while *the latter* is more likely to produce inside matchups.

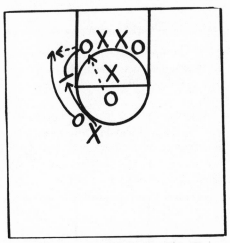

Diag. 169 Offensing The Tip

The only question a coach should have concerning defensing jump balls at the offensive end of the court is, how much territory must be conceded to prevent the opponents from forming a fast break if, or when, they win the tip? If the outcome of the tip is in doubt, the forwards might be arranged as shown in Diagram 170, with two of them back to cover the direct tip toward the opponents' basket.

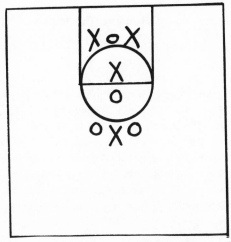

Diag. 170 Defensing The Backcourt Tip

If the outcome of the tip is in doubt, as far as the guards who are flanking the inside forward are concerned, they will *have* to use this type of coverage, or risk an unfavorable one-on-one confrontation inside if the offense wins the tip.

However, if losing the tip is a foregone conclusion, an alignment similar to that of Diagram 171 should prove more effective. Forwards must be alert for screens as they begin retreating downcourt. In other words, if a player cannot win the tip, at least she should not allow her opponents the chance to fast break too.

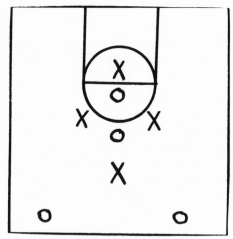

Diag. 171   Defensing The Forecourt Tip

DEFENSING THE FAST BREAK

Fast breaking is the most potent offensive weapon available to a team. It scores points quickly from high percentage shooting areas, keeps constant pressure on the opponents, and often is capable of forcing a team out of its basic style of play. If a team is known as a fast breaking team, the opponents are likely to adjust their game strategy or playing tempo accordingly, except when they feel that their own style is superior.

A further advantage in fast breaking is that certain defenses such as combination zones, trapping, matching, sinking, switching, or pressing are useless in combatting the fast break. A team may be devastating its opponents with a Triangle-One zone, but when the other team gets the ball and initiates a fast break, the guards have no more than three seconds to block the passing lanes or stop the dribble before the forwards assume complete control of the break. Until the opponents' progress toward their goal is slowed down, all other considerations are secondary to the physical act of getting back downcourt on defense as quickly as possible, and stopping the progress of the ball.

It should be apparent, then, that the most favorable time to deal with the fast break is during the early moments of its formation, or even prior to its inception. When confronted with the likelihood of opponents using the fast break to establish the tempo of the game, a team's first consideration should be to reduce the opponents' rebounding superiority, or at least to increase the pressure applied to their best rebounders.

One way to combat the opponents' board strength is to send more forwards to the offensive boards. Of course, the opponents' fast breaking possibilities are greatly enhanced whenever this strategy fails, so a team should have a definite plan of attack in mind. Sending *three* forwards to the boards, for example, (two to double-team the best defensive rebounder, one to go after the ball on her own), while the fourth forward drops back to cover outlet passes or guards the ballhandler as she nears midcourt.

Another way of slowing down the fast break is to send two, or even three, players back downcourt, thereby further weakening the offensive rebounding, but strengthening the chances of stopping the fast break.

Regardless of the method used in combatting the break initially, once in progress it is extremely difficult to stop until it reaches the other end of the court. The middle portion of the fast break, consisting of the forwards' moving the ball downcourt as the guards retreat, is seldom stopped except when a forward relaxes and allows herself to be hemmed in at the sideline. Since most forwards move toward the middle of the court as soon as possible after receiving a pass during the fast break, however, sideline trapping is applicable in theory, but unrealistic in practice.

Defensing fast break situations is seldom easy. However, it is invariably easier in girls' six-player basketball, where two stationary guards are always in position to defense the break, than in boys' ball, where there are no stationary players. The most difficult break to defense is the two-on-one, and due to the omnipresence of *two* stationary guards, such situations are so rare in girls' basketball as to be practically nonexistent. The only frequently encountered fast breaking situations are the four-on-three, three-on-three, four-on-two, and three-on-two.

THE FOUR-ON-THREE FAST BREAK

The four-on-three fast break is likely to occur when a team has two good rebounding stationary guards and two fast rovers, and when three forwards go after the offensive rebound. As shown in Diagram 172, one of the rovers slides to the sideline to receive the outlet pass, while the other moves to the top of the circle or beyond. The rebounder may pass to either of the rovers, but the one at the sideline will always be the trailer, or trailing forward.

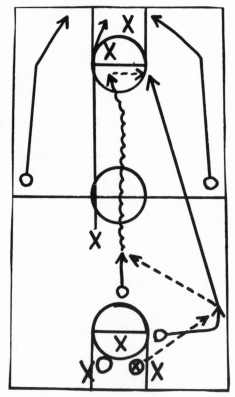

Diag. 172 The Four-on-Three Fast Break

For best results, the point guard should be a stationary guard, and her responsibility is stopping the dribbler's advance. Generally, she should not stop the dribbler beyond the top of the circle, because the other forwards in the break will have a three-on-two or two-on-one advantage if she does not drop back to help out inside after stopping the ball outside.

If the defense manages to get three guards back to stop the break, the third guard should assume one of the inside defensive positions rather than trying to become the point guard. If all three guards do their share–the point stopping the dribbler, the inside guards covering the wing forwards–the shooter will likely be the trailer which, although undesirable, is preferable to an inside shot.

THE THREE-ON-THREE FAST BREAK

The three-on-three situation qualifies as a fast break only in the speed with which the offense moves the ball downcourt. It is best defensed by a basic or matchup diamond two-on, or a one-two zone. In order to simplify the task of stopping the ball, it usually is the latter. The only offensive maneuver off the three-on-three break that might cause trouble is screening, (e.g., the pass-and-cut as was shown in Diagram 160), but even this pattern is unlikely to work against adequate zone coverage.

THE FOUR-ON-TWO FAST BREAK

Four-on-two fast break situations are relatively rare in girls' basketball. When they occur, they are usually the result of a combination of all four forwards going after the rebound, failing to get it, and two guards slipping outside to receive the outlet pass. There is little to say about a four-on-two situation, besides stopping the dribbler and dropping back to cover the inside pass.

THE THREE-ON-TWO FAST BREAK

The most prevalent of all fast-breaking situations in girls' basketball, the three-on-two situation also provides the greatest opportunity for creative, attacking defense. A good fast-breaking team will normally have four to ten, three-on-two breaks per game over a season. *Twenty* potential points per game from fast-breaking alone should be enough to make a coach spend extra practice time developing such a system and working on ways to deny the opponents that kind of advantage.

The three-on-two fast break usually occurs in this manner. Guard X6 pulls down the rebound of an opponent's missed shot, and immediately pivots away from the basket and looks for a teammate breaking downcourt. She clears to the side with one or two dribbles then, spotting teammate X4 breaking down the middle, she throws a baseball pass to X4. Stationary forwards X1 and X2, playing wide at the midcourt corners, advance toward the baseline, cutting to the basket when they reach a point even with an extended free throw line. X4 advances the ball down the middle of the court until stopped by an opponent, then passes to one of the wings who either shoots or passes to the other wing for a layup.

As soon as the stationary guards see the fast break forming, they should retreat to their basic positions and wait for the forwards to come to them. They should be lined up one in front of the other, as shown in Diagram 173, rather than side-by-side. The point guard may set up anywhere from the free throw line to the top of the circle, depending upon her speed and defensive ability, while the inside guard should occupy a position inside the lane between the basket and the edge of the free throw circle.

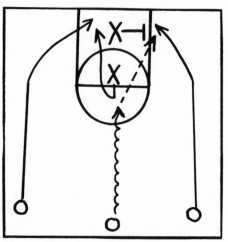

Diag. 173   Defensing The Three-on-Two Fast Break

The point guard's first responsibility is *stopping the dribbler's progress*. She does this by waiting until the dribbler is in the vicinity of the top of the circle, then taking a single, forceful step toward her. She must endeavor to make the step appear to be a genuine effort to guard her, or else the dribbler may continue advancing until she *has* to guard her, in which case she will never be able to retreat in time to stop the opponents from going two-on-one with the inside forward.

If she is successful, the dribbler will catch the ball and pass to a wing, and the point guard should then retreat quickly to cover the wing away from the ball. The inside guard will cover the dribbler's pass to either wing.

When the guards have properly performed their functions, the only open shooting area should be in the vicinity of the free throw line. If the other guards are hustling back downcourt, it should only be open momentarily. If the forwards are forced to take the outside shot or to make more than two passes (dribbler-to-wing and wing-to-other-wing), the stationary guards should be considered as having succeeded in upsetting the fast break, even if the offense subsequently scores. The stationary guards' tasks are to stop the layup and slow down the offense until the rovers can get back and set up.

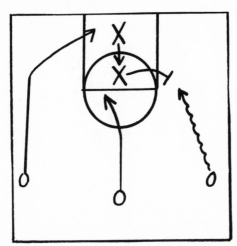

Diag. 174   Defensing The 3-on-2 Fast Break, Ball Coming Up The Side

When the ball comes up the sideline rather than in the middle, the guards' task is slightly easier because one guard can defense the ballhandler while the other guard defenses *both* of the other forwards. (Diagram 174)

The point guard picks up the dribbler as before, and the inside guard moves out to a point roughly equidistant from the other two guards. She should not commit herself defensively to either opponent while the ball is at the sideline, except to break in front of an opponent to intercept a pass. Better guards seldom commit themselves prematurely. They may *fake* aggressive movements, but they will only commit themselves to a given defensive strategy when the forward either commits herself or moves close enough to the basket to force coverage.

6
Zone Defensive Team Techniques

If there is any truth to the old adage that "God must have loved common people, since he made so many of them," the same might be said for zone defenses and their use. In a sense, all zone defenses are ultimately player-to-player defenses, but zones tend to force those confrontations farther out from the basket than do basic player-to-player coverages.

Although the positive reasons for using zone defenses have already been noted, perhaps too little attention has been paid to the reasons why a zone might *not* solve a team's problems:

1. That a zone defense may hide a team's defensive problems is well known; what is not so well understood is that playing zone defense will in no way solve those problems. They will remain, partially or wholly submerged like the business end of an iceberg, and a good team will discover and attack them sooner or later. Meanwhile, the zone will apparently succeed in some cases, thereby reinforcing the likelihood of its future usage.

The point of these rambling thoughts is that young or inexperienced players should learn player-to-player defensive techniques before playing zone defense. Without such experience, they will likely be ineffectual in *any* defensive alignment or strategy, zone or player-to-player. Zone defense is not a panacea for weaknesses. It is, or should be, a tool for attacking specific offensive strengths or weaknesses.

2. Every zone defense has weaknesses, from the 2–2 zone defense thrown to a team by a careless coach who has heard somewhere that that type of zone is easy to learn, to the trapping zones imposed upon an

175

inexperienced team by a coach who blithely assumes that the tougher the defense is to learn, the better his team will play it. The weaknesses may not be readily apparent, but they exist even in such advanced techniques as matching up or trapping. The secret is to find a zone that complements the team's basic strategy—for example, shutting off the opponents' inside game, increasing defensive rebounding strength, or double-teaming an outstanding forward—without yielding the offensive advantage a team might have against a player-to-player defense.

3. Many coaches labor under the misconception that zone defenses are easier to coach than player-to-player defense, while nothing could be further from the truth. Precisely because zones *do* have inherent weaknesses, the coach's task is made more difficult. While it is true that the guards' range of movement is lessened to some extent, and at times even the number of movements is reduced when playing zone defense rather than player-to-player, the possibility of mental error is far greater in the former, especially when the opponents use a continuity offensive pattern involving cutters. Guarding another player is a fact, an actuality, as one can see the body, and follow it to the ends of the earth. On the other hand, guarding a zone, a spot on the floor, an area of the court, is abstract and unreal. It asks you to picture in your mind, situations in which players could enter your zone and score, and then guarding against those possibilities.

Players usually ''get the hang of it'' rather easily, of course. But their first impression is that zone defense is easier to play than player-to-player because it does not tire them out as much. This is a notion as incongruous as the original idea that girls should not play basketball in the first place!

A zone defense that is easy to coach is a zone defense that is easy to beat. Of course, outstanding players can make any defense look easy, but then we are talking about the players rather than the defense itself. As will be made abundantly clear in the following chapters, playing defense well is rarely easy, and a team uses a zone defense for the wrong purpose if it expects to win games through lessened efforts.

The 1–2–1 (Diamond) Zone Defense

The 1–2–1 is probably the most effective and versatile of all zone defenses. In fact, it can be superior even to player-to-player defense in the number and variety of problems it poses for the offense. Some of its advantages are:

1. It features three guards in constant defensive rebounding position, enhancing its value to small teams;

2. It is difficult to achieve offensive penetration inside the lane with the ball;

3. It adapts well as a trapping or matching defense, in addition to its basic usage;

4. Individual defensive responsibilities within any of its three forms are easily learned;

5. The area of the court in which the 1–2–1's coverage is weakest (the corner) is also the part of the court where shooting and passing is most difficult; and

6. The forwards' shooting and passing angles are decreased against a 1–2–1 zone, as opposed to other zones such as the 2–2.

PERSONNEL REQUIREMENTS

In the 1–2–1 zone alignment shown in Diagram 175, X1 is the *point guard,* X2 and X3 are referred to as the *wing guards,* and X4 is the *inside,* or *middle* guard.

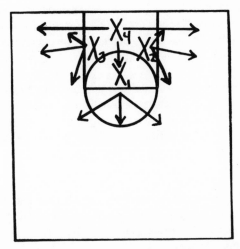

Diag. 175   Basic 1–2–1 Zone Movements

The point guard should be quick, confident, consistent, and aggressive. She must be able to stop the opponents' fast break and drives. She is in a position to be the team's defensive leader, since her initial movements often dictate her teammates' movements and adjustments. The point guard's position is the most difficult defensive position to fill.

Either the inside guard or the wing guard position X3 should be the next position considered, depending upon what position the coach wants the team's best defensive rebounder to play. The rebounder should occupy whatever of the two positions does *not* have responsibility for covering passes to the corner, although the best rebounding position in the basic 1–2–1 is the X3 wing position. The majority of all basketball players are right-handed, and will dribble and shoot from the right side of the offensive court, making the X3 position ideal for overshots and shots angling off the rim or backboard.

Wing position X2 requires a guard who can control the ballhandler. She should be able to play aggressive defense without fouling, since much of the offensive action is likely to occur on her side of the court. When the ball is on the opposite side of the court, her responsibility is the deeper offside forward, as there will only be one offside forward in overload offenses.

An extremely effective alignment is to use the team's best small defender at point guard, a tall girl at X4 covering the corner, the best rebounder at position X3, and use X1/X4 as stationary guards. Such an arrangement will make the team's defensive task easier, since their basic positions are identical to the positions they will occupy in stopping the fast break.

Although the basic 1–2–1 defense appears complicated at first, its movements and responsibilities are usually absorbed quickly by players on all levels. In addition, its strength in stopping or double-teaming inside penetrations make it superior to the 2–2 or other zones defenses, especially with young or inexperienced players.

The Basic 1–2–1 Defense

Matchup zones should be used only when the matchups favor the defense. However, many teams unknowingly use the 1–2–1 as a matchup zone when they would be better suited to the basic form, which definitely is *not* a matchup zone.

For those who are interested in the basic 1–2–1, however, there is good news and bad news. The good news is that the basic form is easy to learn in terms of individual responsibility, an important consideration for coaches with young or inexperienced players, but the bad news is that the basic 1–2–1 zone has weaknesses that a good offense can exploit.

The basic positions in the 1–2–1, those occupied by each of the guards with the ball outside at the middle of the halfcourt, are as follows: X1 should be at, or just outside, the center of the free throw line; X2/X3 should be near the side of the free throw line approximately even with the second free throw space; and X4 should be at the middle of the free throw lane, one step out from the basket. The basic 1–2–1 zone is best suited to teams with height or speed problems, guards who do not defend well in one-on-one matchups, or teams weak inside defensively.

Guard X1 is responsible for covering the ballhandler when the offensive team brings the ball downcourt or sets up in their offensive alignment, regardless of whether the ball comes up either side or the middle of the court. She may have to switch defensive responsibilities if the offense overloads one side of the court, but at this point in time all she needs to know is that she is responsible for stopping the dribbler.

X4 covers the center of the lane when the ball is at the top of the circle, and she covers passes to the baseline, bothering the shooter and stopping baseline drives. In the corner, the dribbler should be encouraged or allowed to dribble toward the middle, where she can be double-teamed by X4 and X2 or X3. If X4 is expected to cover the corner passes, she will have to "cheat" toward the corner as the ball moves away from the center of the court. If not, she will be unable to get to the corner forward in time to guard her adequately. When the ball is outside on either side of the court, X4 should be at the edge of the lane.

A variation of the above can be achieved by having X2 or X3 cover the corner passes instead of X4. Such an arrangement makes X4's job more difficult in terms of responsibility and learning facility, but it can be ideal for teams with one tall rebounding guard. The inside guard X4 will be able to remain in rebounding position regardless of the position of the ball, by having X2 and X3 cover the corners. The two corner coverages are shown in Diagrams 176–177.

Diag. 176 X4 Covering The Corner Pass, Basic 1–2–1 Zone

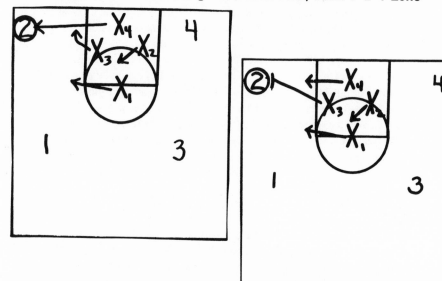

Diag. 177 X3 Covering The Corner Pass, Basic 1–2–1 Zone

Returning to the basic 1–2–1, if the point guard (X1) assumes responsibility of the ball, then X2 and X3 will be responsible for the forwards on either side of the dribbler, with X4 taking the other forward. Thus, if dribbler O1 brings the ball downcourt and passes to teammate O2 as shown in Diagram 178, the entire defense will shift toward the ballside of the court. At the moment, they happen to be matched up with the forwards, and they will stay in their matchups as long as the forwards stay outside.

Overloads such as the one shown in Diagram 179 present no difficulties for the 1–2–1; in fact, ballside overloads inadvertently play to the strength of the basic 1–2–1 by facilitating the inside double-team.

The only weakness in the basic 1–2–1 is matching up when the point guard is responsible for the ballhandler as the offense sets up, and when

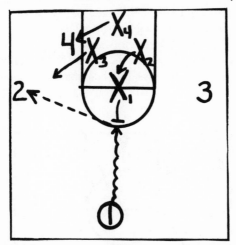

Diag. 178   Defensive Responsibilities After The First Pass, Basic 1–2–1 Zone

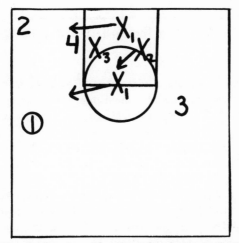

Diag. 179   Defensing The Overload, Basic 1–2–1 Zone

that forward sets up with the ball outside and away from the overload. (Diagram 180) With X1 covering the ball, X2 has no one to guard, but X3 and X4 have to guard three forwards. Sometimes the forwards inadvertently solve the problem for the defense by O1's failing to move to the corner of the lane for the pass, or X1 commits herself to guarding O3, allowing X1 to switch to O1 without giving up the shot from the free throw line.

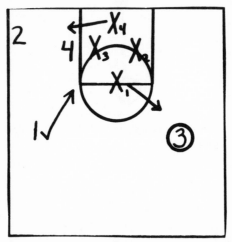

Diag. 180 Attacking The Basic 1–2–1 Zone Weakness

There are three ways to deal with this problem. They include switching to a matchup zone, rotating into a momentary matchup that will still be played as a basic 1–2–1 after the defensive rotation occurs, or leaving it as it is.

All X1 has to do to go into a matchup zone is call "Switch," point with her left hand to O3, then move to her right to guard O1. X2 will be then responsible for guarding O3.

A situation that often causes the guards trouble in the basic 1–2–1 is when the ball is in the corner in an overload offense. (Diagram 181) If X3 needs help guarding O4 at low post, X2 will have to help out, leaving O3 open at the corner of the free throw line. The only possible line of defense in this situation is for X1 to be responsible for O1 and O3, as long as she stays outside. If the corner forward passes to O3, X1 will pick her up, with X3 moving up to cover O1.

Although possibly more difficult to learn, the rotation pattern adapts better to basic 1–2–1 defense than does matching up. After all, if a team merely seeks matchups, it does not need the basic style. Keying the defensive rotation is possibly best done by the free guard (X2), who has no defensive responsibility in Diagram 181 above. Finding that she has no one to guard, she calls out ''shift,'' then moves across the lane to become the new X3. X3 moves to the free throw line, becoming the new X1, while the old X1 guarding O3 becomes X2.

The third choice, X1 guarding both O1 and O3, can be the best decision when (a) X1 is outstanding defensively, (b) either O1 or O3 is a poor shooter or ballhandler, or (c) the offense relies heavily upon inside scoring.

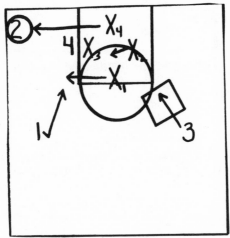

Diag. 181   Offensive Overload With Ball In Corner

When the ball is in the corner, either X3 or X4 covers the ballhandler. X1 is responsible for guarding against inside penetration by outside forwards on the ballside of the court, and in such a position she is often able to double-team the low post, and even triple-team her when the corner guard drops back after the pass. X1's primary responsibility remains defensing the cutters, however.

Whenever possible, the offensive low post (O4 in Diagram 182) should be guarded toward the inside of the court.

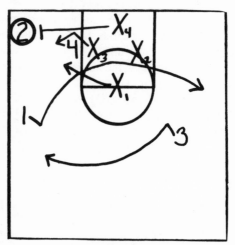

Diag. 182   Defensing The Inside Pass From The Corner, Basic 1–2–1 Zone

USING THE 1–2–1 ZONE AS A MATCHUP ZONE

If the basic 1–2–1 zone appears complicated, but is actually easy to learn, the exact opposite is true of the 1–2–1 zone adapted to matching up. Anyone can match up, but doing it without surrendering defensive control requires awareness of the opponents' offensive strengths and weaknesses, as well as superior skills in individual defensive fundamentals.

The easiest way to match up within *any* zone defense is for the coach to have previously scouted the opponents, chart the team's basic offensive plays, and note the players who occupy each position. Armed with that information, the coach assigns each guard responsibility for a single forward within the team's zone defense.

Therefore, matchups consist of any offensive or defensive movements that result in one-on-one situations. When a team uses such movements within a zone defense as a team strategy in controlling their opponent, they are said to be using a matchup zone.

A strange paradox concerning the use of matchup zones is that a 2–2 zone matchup will almost always shift into a 1–2–1 alignment, while a 1–2–1 zone will invariably matchup 2–2. The reason for this is shown in Diagram 183 and is known offensively as splitting the defense. When a team sets up in any given zone, the opponents are likely to set up offensively in areas of the court along the edges, or seams, of the zone.

Diag. 183 Matching Up Against A 2–2 Zone Offense

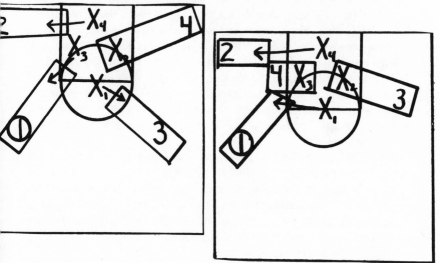

Diag. 184 Matching Up Against An Overload Offense, 1–2–1 Zone

Splitting patterns will not work against matchup zones, however, because the guards will merely shift into whatever alignment the offense is set up. (They will still be in a 1–2–1 zone, whether they remain in the

1–2–1 alignment or not.) Thus, the offense will have to attack the player-to-player aspects of a zone defense and, because the defense will only matchup when it is to *their* advantage to do so, the offense is likely to be given a full test of its capabilities.

With defensive superiority established, a matchup zone is clearly superior to a basic zone. Where the defensive personnel is skilled enough to matchup with their opponents, the matchup zone is the most difficult defense to attack in basketball. It is even more difficult than a good player-to-player defense, since the matchup essentially is player-to-player defense with the added protection of a zone. The team that matches up is likely to be outstanding defensively, since it requires greater concentration, alertness, and reactions than other types of zones. When guards are in foul trouble, or when they cannot contain their forwards one-on-one, the team should change to a more basic defensive attack.

The number one priority in implementing a matchup zone is stopping the opponents' inside game. If Team A plays Team B ten times, and stops their inside game defensively in eight games, they will be very unlikely to lose more than three of the ten games. Outside shooting does not win games, at least, not on a regular basis. The team that wins is the team that can penetrate offensively for high-percentage shots like short jumpers, hooks, layups, or tipins, while forcing their opponents to shoot from outside.

To be successful, a matchup zone must deny the forwards high-percentage shots and offensive rebounds, and the keys to success are defensive strength inside and stopping the offensive drives to the basket. In order to control inside forwards, the guards should either be proficient at blocking shots, or capable of keeping the ball away from inside forwards via overguarding or fronting. Of the two, the latter is by far the easier technique to master.

Where driving is concerned, the guard should attempt to force the dribbler toward the middle of the court without losing defensive control. The dribbler should never be allowed to drive the baseline. Finally, if all else fails, the guard should give up an outside shot rather than a layup, operating under the assumption that a shot taken from twelve feet out is harder to make than a shot from six feet, and a shot from six feet out is more difficult than one from three feet. A girl who says she can shoot better from distances of 15–25 feet probably *can* shoot with more accuracy from those distances, but what she is *really* saying is "I can't shoot well with somebody guarding me." With close defensive pressure, she is unlikely to shoot well from anywhere on the court.

Matching up will not work when the one-on-one confrontations favor the forwards, and it is this fact that makes the matchup zone difficult to operate against certain teams. When the defense matches up, they have already determined the most favorable matchups and considered the consequences of that strategy, and when the forwards shift or pass through the lane as cutters, the guards will not follow them beyond the limits of their zones, or they would be in a player-to-player defense. These cutting movements create new matchups that may or may not be to the guards' advantage, and when the offensive pattern calls for multiple cutting movements across the zone boundaries, the guards can become so absorbed in changing defensive responsibilities that they cannot adequately protect their zones from offensive penetration.

Aggressive, experienced guards can usually adapt to such movements with a minimal loss of efficency, but whenever they lose defensive control they should return to the basic zone strategy.

USING THE 1–2–1 ZONE AS A TRAPPING ZONE

While the 2–2 zone is more effective in trapping the ball at the top of the circle, the 1–2–1 zone is decidedly superior when the trap is sprung in the corner. Corner trapping has the extra advantage of reducing the number of passing lanes and/or escape routes available to the ballhandler, and, also, the offensive advantage of layups or other high-percentage shots when the trap fails to contain the ball.

Therefore, teams are usually highly selective about who and when they trap in the corner. If they are not selective, the offense may send its best ballhandler to the baseline and, after the trapping guards commit themselves, she will merely pass the ball to a teammate for a three-on-two offensive advantage. Good ballhandlers should not be trapped, and a team should not trap automatically everytime a forward dribbles to the baseline. Success in trapping usually depends on surprising the ballhandler, then forcing her into a dribbling or passing mistake before she can recover her poise. There are two aspects of trapping, covering the ballhandler and blocking the passing lanes.

1. *Covering the Ballhandler.* A typical trapping situation begins with

a forward, O3 in Diagram 185, dribbling toward the baseline, guarded loosely by X2. As O3 nears the seam in the zone, X4 moves out to pick her up at the baseline.* At this point X2 usually drops back to defense the inside pass. X2 retreats slightly, but as the ballhandler reaches the corner and X4 exerts defensive pressure, X2 moves quickly toward O3's blind side. (If the dribbler stops or changes direction before reaching the corner, she should not be trapped.)

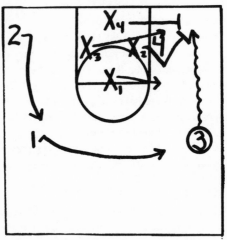

Diag. 185   1–2–1 Zone Trapping In The Corner

If the guards' objective is to steal the ball while O3 is dribbling, X4 will move in low and turn O3 away from the baseline and toward X2, who will attempt to steal the ball off the dribble. If their goal is to stop the dribbler and force a bad pass, X4 will keep her hands high, waving them around, while X2 similarly distracts the ballhandler's attention and tries to deflect the ball if O3 brings it low in an unguarded position.

The greatest danger to the defense during trapping is the inside pass. X4 must have quick hands and long arms to discourage such attempts. Only when the defense can eliminate the possibility of the inside pass can they hope to steal the ball or force turnovers much of the time.

*Corner trapping can occur only from the coverage shown in Diagram 185, with X4 covering the corners. It will not work with X3 covering the baseline.

2. *Covering The Other Forwards.* Most of a team's success in corner trapping with the 1–2–1 zone will be due to the efforts of X2 and X4 in containing the ball or forcing bad passes. If O3 makes a good pass, the offense will likely score regardless of the efforts of X1 or X3. The best X1 or X3 can do is to know the location of the passing lanes, and bisect the angle of O3's most likely passes. X3 covers inside passes. If X2 and X4 do their jobs adequately, the only inside passing lane open will be between X2 and X4, and X3 should be positioned there. (Diagram 185)

X1 covers the outside passes and, since she cannot hope to cover the entire court, her best position is approximately at the corner of the free throw lane. The two most likely outside passing lanes are to a forward deep on the ballside of the court (O1 in Diagram 185), or the risky crosscourt pass to O2 at the offside corner of the lane. X1's intermediate position, while not guaranteeing that she will intercept O3's outside pass if it occurs, will at least ensure that the guards will have time to return to their basic defensive positions before the offense can attack.

When used judiciously, trapping can serve to keep a team off balance offensively, disrupting their patterns and their composure. It requires a great deal of teamwork, quickness, and timing, but with aggressive, determined guards harassing the ballhandler, it is a formidable defensive weapon.

The 2–2 Zone Defense

The 2–2 is the most widely used of all zone defenses in girls' basketball. It is, in fact, as basic to girls' basketball as player-to-player defense. Beyond the fact that its basic movements and responsibilities are easily understood by players on all levels of play, it is also true that sooner or later every zone defense becomes a 2–2 zone.

Aside from initial facility in teaching and learning, however, there are few advantages in a 2–2 alignment. Outside trapping at the top of the circle is easier from a 2–2 or 2–1–1 alignment than from defenses featuring a point guard, and teams with specific defensive strengths (e.g., two short, quick guards, or strong rebounding), might profit from a 2–2 zone. Its widespread usage, however, is perhaps more a matter of tradition or expediency than indicative of its true value.

For example, the 2–2 zone is weak inside. Due to the presence of a spot in the center of the free throw lane where all four guards' responsibilities overlap (Diagram 186), there is often confusion concerning which guard has the responsibility for covering inside cutters. In the 1–2–1 or 1–3 zones, this problem is usually solved by having X4 cover *all* inside cutters.

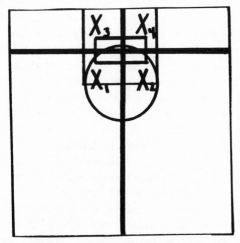

Diag. 186   Basic 2–2 Zone, Individual Responsibilities

A second problem in using the 2–2 is that outside splitting is more likely to yield high-percentage outside shots than, say, the 1–2–1 zone, that gives up the corner shot rather than the forty-five to sixty degree shooting angle usually achieved against a 2–2. Furthermore, because the action occurs away from the corners, the ballhandler usually has more passing lanes available.

BASIC 2–2 ZONE DEFENSE

In the 2–2 zone's basic form, most of the defensive pressure is on the outside guards, who must stop the ball, then drop back to cover whichever outside wing forward receives the pass. Few teams use this method, however, since the guards' movements toward the ball render unlikely the prospect of their retreating to cover the pass to the wing. If the outside guards cover the wing passes, the wing forwards will set up lower, or nearer the baseline. If the inside guards cover the wing passes, the wing forwards will set up higher.

Diag. 187   Basic 2–2 Zone Defense

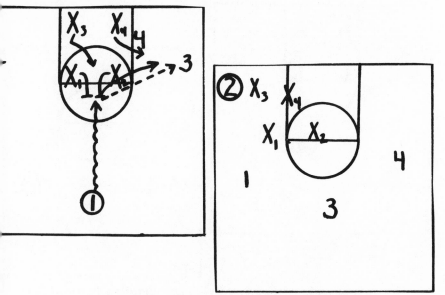

Diag. 188   Basic 2–2 Zone, Ball In Corner

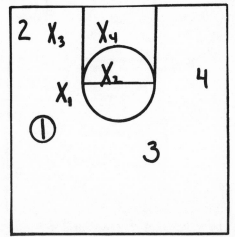

Diag. 189   Basic 2–2 Zone, Ball Outside

Diag. 190   Basic 2–2 Zone, Ball At Point

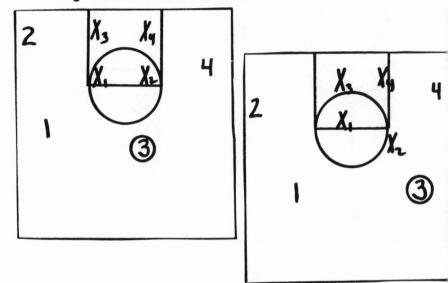

Diag. 191   Basic 2–2 Zone, Ball Rotating To Right Side

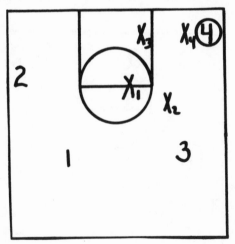

Diag. 192   Basic 2–2 Zone, Ball In Right Corner

A better use of the basic 2–2 zone is found in trapping the point forward as she dribbles outside or advances the ball. The outside guards' movements are the same as in the basic techniques, except that instead of bluffing a movement toward the ball and retreating to cover the pass to the wing, the outside guards move up quickly to double-team the dribbler. The guard then, on whichever side the ballhandler is dribbling, attempts to turn the dribbler into the other outside guard.

As with all trapping movements, surprise is vital if the defense is to not only stop the dribbler, but also, steal the ball or force a bad pass.

MATCHING UP IN THE 2–2 ZONE DEFENSE

There are two ways to match up defensively in the 2–2 zone. A team can play basic defense, with both outside guards stopping the point forward's advance and the *inside* guards covering the wing passes, or they can match up before the point forward makes the pass to the wing. Of the two, matching up *before* the pass to the wing is preferable in defensing teams with strong outside shooting, while matching up after the wing pass tends to protect the inside in favor of yielding the outside shot.

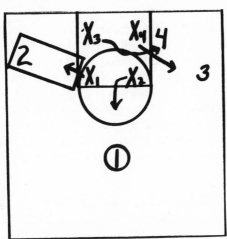

Diag. 193   2–2 Zone Matchup Occurring *Before* The Pass To The Wing

Diag. 194 2–2 Zone Matchup, X1 Covering Point Forward O1 Before Pass

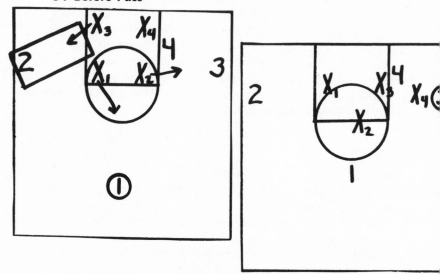

Diag. 195 2–2 Zone Matchup *After* **The Pass To The Wing**

Whenever the opponents have been scouted prior to playing them, the guards should know (a) the offensive alignments from which their opponents usually attack a 2–2 zone; (b) that method of matching up will likely be more successful against them; and (c) their own individual assignments (e.g., overguarding, sinking, fronting, etc.) once the matchup is achieved. Matching up should never be based on guesswork. Even when the information in (a) is not readily available, the guards should follow a coordinated, cohesive plan of attack that is thoroughly understood by everyone involved in the defensive effort.

TRAPPING FROM A 2–2 ZONE

The basic 2–2 zone is strongest in defensing the shot from the top of the circle or the pass to the high post. It can also provide trapping strength at the top of the circle, although it is not usually effective in trapping elsewhere.

Like 1–2–1 trapping, 2–2 trapping should not be used indiscriminately. It is not a "gimmick" defense used to hide some kind of defensive weakness, it is an authentic attacking defense that requires fast, experienced outside guards, teamwork, and excellent timing. Only three types of situations are likely to produce conditions favorable to trapping at the point in the 2–2 zone:

1. When the point forward is inexperienced, a poor dribbler or passer, or hesitant in moving the ball, the outside guards may be able to set up farther out than usual and trap her before she is ready to pass the ball. (Diagram 196) The inside guards should also play farther out from the

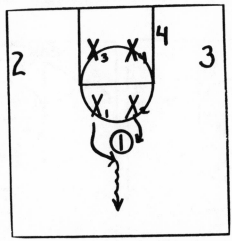

Diag. 196   Trapping At The Point, 2–2 Zone

basket until the wing pass is made, since the ballhandler is unlikely to complete the inside pass with two guards harassing her. The trapping movement is the same as in the 1–2–1, with one guard turning the dribbler while the other outside guard moves in from the dribbler's blind side to steal the ball. If the point forward completes the pass to, say, wing O3, X4 will cover her, X3 will drop low to cover O4, and X1 must drop back to guard O2.

2. When the point forward is the opponents' only good ballhandler, or when she tends to dribble more than she ought to, she can sometimes be lured into trapping situations. This is done by overguarding her to stop her

lateral progress, then turning her as before and going after the ball before she can catch it. Trapping a good ballhandler entails greater risks than with weaker forwards however, and the outside guards must not set the trap too far outside lest they be unable to get back quickly when the ballhandler completes the pass to a wing for a three-on-two offensive advantage.

When they are unsuccessful in stealing the ball, the trapping guards must prevent the inside pass at all costs. If the pass is made to a wing forward at the sideline, the three-on-two will be far less effective than it is when the ballhandler is at the middle of the offensive court. (Diagrams 197–198.)

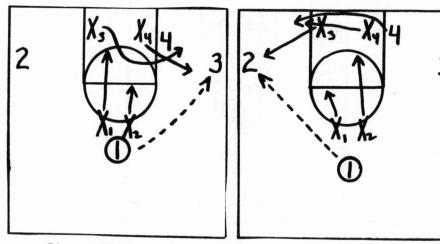

Diag. 197–198   Defensive Rotation When Outside Trapping Fails To Contain The Ball

3. Offenses featuring the point forward's challenging the outside guards (Diagram 199) are sometimes susceptible to trapping, although situations should be chosen carefully because the element of surprise is missing. When ballhandler O1 consciously dribbles into two guards to force double-coverage, she is hardly likely to be caught unaware by their efforts to trap her. The possibility exists, however, and should be taken into consideration in defensing such offensive tactics.

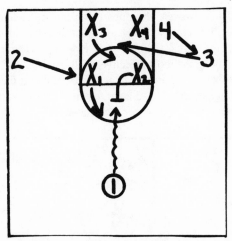

Diag. 199   Trapping In Offensive Penetration Attempt, 2–2 Zone

The 1–1–2 Zone Defense

The 1–1–2 zone is actually a modified 2–2 zone, strengthened inside by an outside guard's dropping back to form a rebounding triangle with the inside guards. (Diagram 200)

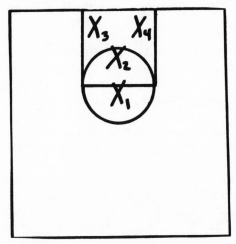

Diag. 200   1–1–2 Zone Defensive Alignment

Unfortunately, however, the apparent increased defensive strength inside is largely illusory, since offensive splitting at the corners of the free throw line will force guard X2 into 2–2 coverage. (Diagram 201) The 1–1–2 can be among the most effective of all zone defenses in matching up, because eleven coaches out of ten will facilitate the matchup by setting up 2–2 against the 1–1–2 zone, trying for the obvious shot at the corner of the lane if the guards do not match up.

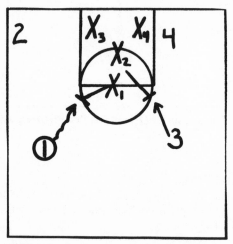

Diag. 201   Offensively Forcing A Matchup From 1–1–2 Zone

The basic zones, whether 2–2, 1–2–1, 1–1–2, or any other, operate under the premise that, once a team is in a particular defense, it retains its basic shape regardless of the position of the ball. In the 1–1–2, for example, inside guard X4 covers the pass to the corner, but to retain the basic shape X2 must cover both the low post and the corner of the free throw line. Although the 1–1–2 matches up as a 2–2 zone (Diagram 201), in its basic form it tends to force double coverage in critical scoring areas. (Diagram 202)

Therefore, it is simpler to matchup with the forwards in the 1–1–2 zone than to maintain its basic shape merely to satisfy theoretical or aesthetic needs. In Diagram 202, all the defense has to do to matchup is send X3 to cover low post O2.

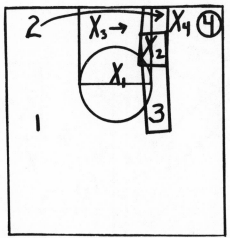

Diag. 202 Basic 1–1–2 Zone, Defensing Ball In Corner

The 2–1–1 Zone Defense

The 2–1–1 zone defense is similar to the 1–1–2, in fact, it *is* the 1–1–2, upside down. As could be expected, it is particularly strong against outside shooting, except the corners, and play around the high post and the top of the circle. Like the 1–1–2 zone, the 2–1–1 zone works better in its matchup defensive rotation than in its basic style. First, the two guards-out alignment is difficult to maintain when the ball is in the corner, and second, quick rotation of the ball will almost invariably yield a clear, high-percentage shot. (Diagrams 203–205.)

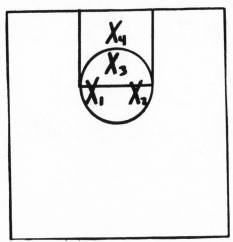

Diag. 203 2–1–1 Zone Defensive Alignment

Diag. 204 Matching Up In The 2–1–1 Zone Defense

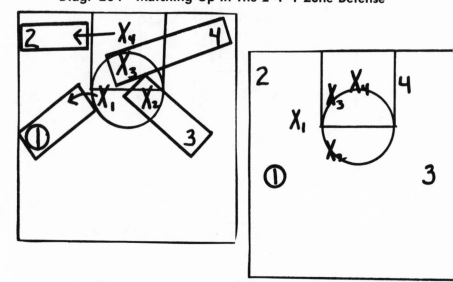

Diag. 205 Basic 2–1–1 Zone Rotation, Ball At Sideline

A team might use a basic 2–1–1 zone defense successfully when the opponents have one superior outside shooter or ballhandler in defensing forwards cutting through the lane, or in trapping the ballhandler at the top of the circle, in which case the 2–1–1 would be played like a 2–2 zone.

The 2–1–1 should not be used against a team with *two* inside scoring threats. When the opponents have two forwards capable of scoring inside, the defense is probably better off in a 1–2–1 or 1–3 zone.

The 1–3 Zone Defense

Although feasible as a matchup defense, the 1–3 zone (Diagram 206) is designed to combat teams with two superior inside scoring threats. In so doing, it tends to give up the outside shot at the corner of the free throw lane, but that risk must be weighed against the danger of single coverage of the inside forwards.

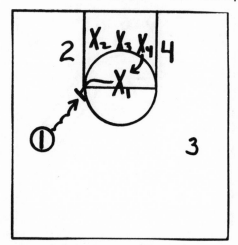

Diag. 206   Basic 1–3 Zone Defense

The 1–3 alignment is inferior to other zone setups in terms of matching up, due to the distance to be covered by whichever guard covers the first pass. In its basic form, however, it rivals the 1–2–1 in the facility with which inside double-teaming can be achieved. The middle inside guard may be positioned at the center of the lane or toward either inside forward, depending upon the situation, individual skills, and team strategy.

In Diagram 207, X1 stops the ball, X3 covers both inside passes with help from X2/X4, and either X1 or X4 will cover the outside pass to O3. If X4 covers the pass to O3, the zone will tend to rotate into a matchup. For the basic 1–3 to be effective, the opponents' outside shooting and ballhandling abilities must be inferior, since point guard X1 will be largely responsible for defensing both O1 and O3. The 1–3 zone can provide effective defensive coverage, but only against certain opponents in specific situations.

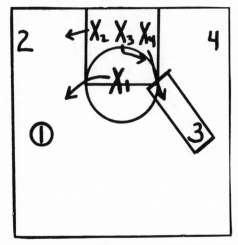

Diag. 207   Matching Up In The 1–3 Zone

The Triangle-One (Combination) Zone Defense

When the opponents have one outstanding forward whose skill may be ballhandling, shooting, or a combination of the two, neither zone nor player-to-player defense may provide adequate coverage to stop her. For example, if she is a good outside shooter who also excels at driving, a zone will tend to give her the outside shot, while single-coverage player-to-player defense will allow her to drive.

Combination defenses (in this case, the triangle-one, since it is the only combination defense in girls' and women's basketball), are designed to deal with just such situations as those described above. The triangle-one offers player-to-player single outside coverage of the best forward with a triangle (1–2 or 2–1) zone double-teaming inside whenever she tries to penetrate.

The triangle-one is most effective against teams with only one good forward, especially an outside forward. It is least effective against teams with balanced scoring or inside play.

The matchups are easily achieved with the ''one'' forward outside.

(Diagram 208) When the "one" forward occupies a low post position as shown in Diagram 209, however, the defense will not be as effective in stopping the outside forwards' penetration. Obviously, the choice of using or not using a triangle-one zone should not be made arbitrarily or flippantly, but should be weighed against the other forwards' scoring abilities, and their tactics against the triangle-one.

Diag. 208 Triangle-One Defensive Matchup With "One" Outside

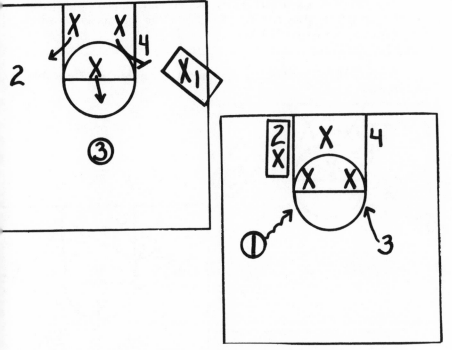

Diag. 209 Triangle-One Defensive Matchup With "One" Inside

In terms of the relative effectiveness of the 1–2 or 2–1 zone, the only pertinent guideline is that *there should never be more forwards inside than guards*. Therefore, if the offense sets up 2–2 as in Diagram 209, with the "one" inside, the only possible defenses are to set up 1–2 hoping to stop the outside guards' penetration, or shift into a 2–2 zone, an undesirable strategy if the best inside forward operates well one-on-one.

Teams with balanced scoring, good outside shooting, or two effective inside forwards will likely beat the triangle-one. For example, let us assume that Team A, the offensive team, has all four forwards averaging between ten to twelve points per game. If Team B uses a triangle-one zone, they will probably hold down one of the opponents, but the other three can overload the opposite side of the court and force the defense into unfavorable one-on-one situations. They could, also, play their regular outside splitting pattern to force the defense into undesirable defensive situations. (Diagrams 210–211)

Diag. 210   Overloading Against A Triangle-One Zone Defense

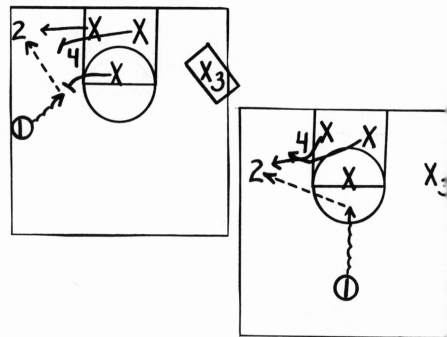

Diag. 211   Forcing One-on-One Against A Triangle-One Zone

In summary, the triangle-one zone is likely to be effective only when much of the opponents' offensive effectiveness derives from the play of one particular forward, or when the offense is forced out of its ordinary playing patterns and into situations favoring the defense.

7
The Presses

The purposes of full or half-court presses are to upset the opponents psychologically, force turnovers, or steal the ball. Within this framework, the guards may attempt any of the following: slowing the forwards' progress (or the downcourt progress of the ball) in order to force ten-second turnovers or run down the clock; using sudden, unexpected traps to steal the ball or harass the ballhandler into hasty, inaccurate passes; forcing the ball away from the opponents' best ballhandlers (usually, the rovers) and toward their poorer ballhandlers (the guards) while the ball is in the opponents' defensive court; or simply applying constant, full-court defensive pressure to wear down the opponents' resistance.

Prerequisites for a successful press include: adequate team speed, especially in retreating when the opponents have beaten the press; aggressive guard play, preferably enhanced by a solid defensive foundation; awareness of the nuances of the particular presses being used (e.g., when and how the trapping situations occur); and proper conditioning to perform the high-speed starting, stopping, and changes-of-direction necessary in pressing defense.

There are disadvantages in using presses. First, if the guards are extremely slow or inexperienced, or if the forwards are outstanding at fast breaking, the opponents are likely to score baskets by fast breaking whenever the press does not work. Also, pressing is questionable in situations involving players in foul trouble. The exception is when circumstances warrant such strategy regardless of foul difficulty, as when a team is slightly behind near the end of the game. Finally, a basic premise of all presses is that, to be successful in pressing, the guards must play more aggressively than the opposing forwards. If the opponents are allowed to attack a pressing defense, they will beat it more often than not. The defense cannot attack the opponents until it counters their offensive attack against the press, and some players simply are not capable of attacking their opponents. In cases where the guards cannot execute aggressive defensive maneuvers without fouling or weakening the team's defensive position, they should drop back and form a more stable defense at the other end of the court.

On the other hand, there is never any acceptable reason why the stationary forwards cannot at least go through the motions of playing defense, since they have nothing better to do as the opponents move downcourt. Whether the rovers drop back or not, the stationary forwards should apply defensive pressure to the ball and to the most likely receiver in that half of the court. If given the opportunity, the dribbler might throw the ball away or commit a dribbling violation or other turnover.

Which Press Should I Use

The best pressing defenses are those that best fit a team's particular needs. Presses may involve the entire court or any part of it, usually half, and they may take the form of either zone or player-to-player defense. Several factors will influence their decision as to which type of press defense and coverage to be used. These factors include:

1. The urgency of the team's need for the ball;
2. The type of bringin coverage desired;
3. The guards' mobility, especially in trapping and covering players away from the ball;
4. The guards' ability to cover and eliminate the threat of the long pass or layup;
5. The opponents' ballhandling patterns, styles, and preferences.

For example, a team only three or four points behind with less than a minute to play should not be using a half-court press. Additionally, the guards should trap the ballhandler in such situations, since regular player-to-player defense is ineffective in stopping the dribbler in most situations. Regular zone coverage, on the other hand, is time-consuming. When a team is a few points behind going into the last minute of a game, they are far more likely to use a trapping defense, either player-to-player or zone.

Where full-court presses are concerned, the defense has three alternative courses of action in defensing the inbounds pass. They can (a) concede the inbounds pass and begin pressing after the pass—a typical zone press strategy; (b) single-guard the forwards player-to-player, including the inbounds passer; or (c) ignore the inbounds passer and double-team the best forward.

Of the three, the least desirable in ordinary circumstances is ignoring the inbounder to double-cover the best forward, because of the danger of the fast break off a return pass to the inbounder, as shown in Diagram 212. Of course, sometimes such coverage is required, but generally it should be avoided.

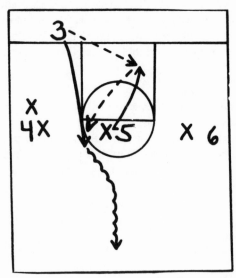

Diag. 212 Fast Breaking Off Double-Coverage, Full-Court Press

The 2–2–2 and 3–1–2 full-court zone presses are the most frequently encountered alignments that do not combat the inbounds pass. In most cases, coverage does not begin until the pass receiver either dribbles or passes the ball. The advantage of not defensing the pass is that once the offensive team has committed itself to one course of action, its alternatives are diminished if the defense can force it away from its primary options and routes. The disadvantage is that the pause can allow the offensive team to organize its attack and control the movement of the ball.

A third factor to be considered in utilizing a team's full-court defensive potential is the mobility of the guards. If they are too slow in dropping back when the opponents break the press; if they are slow or reluctant in trapping or single coverage; of if they cannot control the ballhandler, they should not use a full-court press. Generally speaking, full-court presses attempt to slow down the dribbler's progress and force ten-second violations whenever possible, although trapping defenses are sometimes devastating in terms of stealing the ball when the defense is mobile and aggressive. The closer to its own basket a team regains possession of the ball, the greater their chances of scoring an unmolested layup. If the guards are sound enough defensively to steal the ball a high percentage of the time, they should use a full-court press. Sometimes, however, a team merely wants more time to organize its defensive attack, and the half-court alignment gives them time to regroup before attacking. Unfortunately, however, it also gives the opponents time to prepare their attack. The outstanding feature of half-court presses is the increased defensive pressure brought on by as many as five guards within twelve feet of the half-court line at one time. This is compounded by the presence of four or five offensive players in the same area. With eight to ten players in such a confined area, the possibility of ballhandling errors increases drastically whenever the guards can control the ballhandler and players away from the ball.

Returning to the original contention, the same increased defensive pressure can exist on the full-court level, but only when the guards can control their forwards in one-on-one confrontations. Full-court presses are harder to operate successfully than half-court presses because of the likelihood of spreading the defense, and if the guards are not especially mobile, they can still operate effectively in half-court alignments because of the confusion and congestion of so many players in an overcrowded area of the court. No such overcrowding can occur in full-court pressing, since the forwards can spread to the corners and force matchups favorable to the offense.

The fourth factor in examining pressing possibilities is the defense's ability to combat or eliminate long downcourt passes or fast break situations. Without assurance of such defensive stability, trapping becomes an impossibility, as does the entire range of full-court defense, and possibly half-court pressing as well. A team weak in stopping the offensive advance downcourt should either forget pressing entirely, or keep two guards deep to cover the fast break (e.g., 2–2–2, 3–1–2, 1–2–1–2, etc.)

Finally, a team should consider the opponents' ballhandling patterns, styles, and preferences in determining the most effective pressing defense. For example, if a team depends on one forward to bring the ball across the half-court line, trapping can be extraordinarily successful, as can the simple act of keeping the ball away from the best ballhandler. Or, if the ballhandlers cannot dribble equally well with either hand, a matchup defense that forces them to go to their weak side, then traps them, can yield many steals and subsequent layups. If a team likes to make long downcourt passes, taking those passes away from them can help to frustrate their efforts to move the ball. Against outstanding ballhandling, a half-court press is far more likely to be effective than full-court pressing.

Player-To-Player Presses

Player-to-player full-court presses usually combine pressing and trapping defensive techniques, first, by contesting the inbounds pass, then by pressuring the ballhandler and attempting to lead her into trapping situations. Player-to-player patterns require that all six guards play good defense, and it is imperative that each player be skilled enough to at least slow the dribbler down, if not actually control her. Without controlling the dribbler, the best the defense can hope for is to maintain the matchups, since trapping will be a remote possibility.

Player-to-player pressing is far less effective than zone pressing, except when the guards are able to maintain control of their forwards. When the forwards are pressed player-to-player, they will likely spread out to the corners of the half-court, with the best ballhandler advancing the ball down-court one-on-one. If she is double-teamed, she will pass to an open teammate. Therefore, the greatest value of full-court pressing on a player-to-player basis is likely to be forcing inbounding violations or mistakes.

An ideal trapping situation is to force the best ballhandler to pass the ball away, then increase the defensive pressure on the weaker ballhandlers without allowing the better ballhandler(s) to regain possession of the ball. Full-court presses have the dual objective of stealing the ball or forcing offensive errors, or causing ten-second violations. Forcing the weaker ballhandlers to bring the ball downcourt can achieve either of the two objectives in full-court player-to-player defense.

Half-court player-to-player presses, on the other hand, are rarely seen because they cannot achieve the second objective as effectively as a full-court press, and their zone counterparts are at least as effective in achieving the first objective. If a team plans to use a half-court press, a zone press that matches up with the forwards is probably superior to any type of player-to-player setup.

Full-Court Zone Presses
THE 2–2–2 FULL-COURT PRESS

The chief advantage of the 2–2–2 full-court press is the facility with which its basic positions are learned. The stationary forwards assume the two defensive positions nearest the inbounds passer, the rovers are near midcourt, and the two stationary guards are defensing the opponents' stationary forwards.

The 2–2–2 is most effective in matching up, as shown in Diagram 214. Once the matchup is achieved, the guards may trap whenever they can maneuver the ballhandler into blind double-teaming situations.

In setting the matchups, the guards will defense whatever forward moves into their zone, as shown in Diagrams 213–214. When effective, matching up within the press almost always forces the offense into spreading, or moving to the four corners of the half-court to reduce the possibility of defensive double-teaming.

The stationary forwards should be "cheating" toward whatever side of the basket the inbounder moves to bring the ball in. It is usually to the guards' left, since most ballhandlers prefer to go to their right instead of their left. The rovers line up equidistant from the sidelines in the 2–2–2,

Diag. 213 Forecourt Alignment, 2–2–2 Full-Court Press

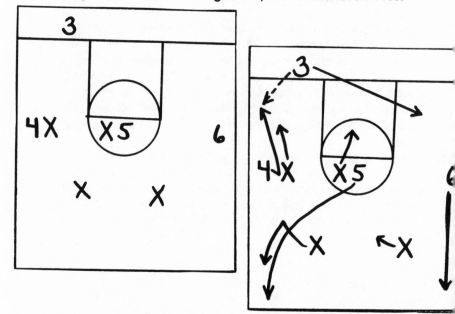

Diag. 214 Matching Up In The 2–2–2 Full-Court Press

but the offside rover will cheat toward the middle of the court whenever the receiver is unlikely to complete the long diagonal pass to her midcourt corner.

The seam between the zones is sometimes vulnerable to offensive attack, and the opponents may use splitting as an adjunct or alternative to spreading patterns. Splitting consists of sending cutters into and through the seam in the zone between the four guards after the inbounds pass has been made. (Diagram 215) Splitting is more likely to occur when the guards trap the pass receiver, but whenever it happens, the ballside rover is responsible for covering the cutter.

Trapping with the 2–2–2 is not easily achieved, except when the ball is passed into the middle of the court, or the forwards are extremely slow or

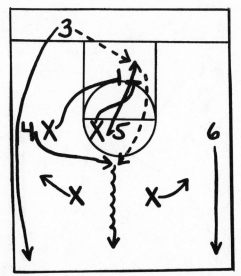

Diag. 215 Splitting The 2–2–2 Full-Court Press When The Guards Trap

poor ballhandlers. Otherwise, there is not enough time for the stationary forwards on defense to double-team the receiver. The trapping forward-guards should wait until the inbounds receiver commits herself by dribbling or passing the ball before instigating trapping movements. Premature trapping almost always yields the long, diagonal pass to the half-court corner, and, subsequently, enhances the opponents' fast-breaking potential.

A frequently encountered trapping strategy is for one guard to stop the dribbler as the other moves in to stop the pass. The initial defense consists of moving in low into an overguarding position that will either stop the dribbler or turn her into the trapping guard. Obviously, it must be done quickly, since the rest of the offensive team has a 3–2 player advantage in that half-court.

When the ball is trapped in the ballside corner (Diagram 216), the rovers move in to cover the most likely passing lanes. They may expose themselves to the long, diagonal crosscourt pass, but if the trap is sprung

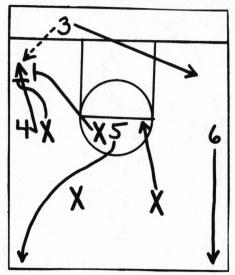

Diag. 216 2–2–2 Trapping In The Ballside Corner

quickly and aggressively enough, the likelihood of those passes being completed will be diminished. Without this assurance, however, the press is likely to break down.

The dilemma of the 2–2–2 full-court press is that, while it favors trapping in the middle of the court (Diagram 217), the area contains more passing lanes than does corner trapping, and a team is more likely to get ''burned'' by the long corner passes in the former.

THE 3–1–2 AND 1–3–2 FULL-COURT PRESSES

These zone presses have an initial advantage over the 2–2–2 press in that they may be used to contest the inbounds pass, whereas the 2–2–2 gives away the bringin to begin defending after the pass is made. This advantage of constant pressure on the ball can cause inbounding errors even when the defensive pressure is not unusually great. Both the 3–1–2 and 1–3–2 full-court presses rotate into 2–2–2 in matching up. (Diagrams 219–220)

The 3–1–2 trap (Diagram 220) is similar to that of the 2–2–2, except it is more effective when the ball is forced away from the corners. As in all

Diag. 217   2–2–2 Trapping In The Middle

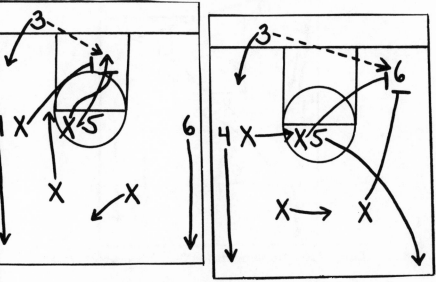

Diag. 218   2–2–2 Trapping In The Offside Corner

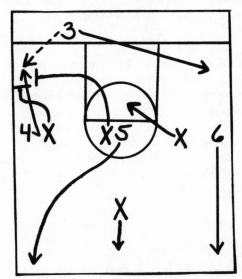

Diag. 219   Matching Up In The 3–1–2 Full-Court Press

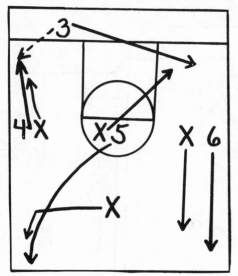

Diag. 220 Trapping In The 3–1–2 Full-Court Press

other full-court presses, the surprise element is the most crucial aspect in combatting the long corner passes since the ''1'' guard has to defend both offside corners in trapping situations in the 3–1–2.

The 1–3–2 full-court press can be the most versatile of all full-court presses. Because many teams set up 1–3–2, it is ideally suited for matching up (Diagram 221), and the guard defending the inbounds pass makes that aspect of the press especially difficult for the offense. Additionally, the position of the guard defending the bringin pass is ideal for trapping the ball in the corner, as shown in Diagram 222. The guard in the middle of the ''3'' covers the crosscourt pass to the inbounder or opposite baseline corner, while the offside guard moves to the midcourt area to guard both midcourt corners.

THE 1–2–1–2 FULL-COURT PRESS

The 1–2–1–2 full-court press is used only infrequently to contest the

Diag. 222 Trapping In The 1–3–2 Full-Court Press

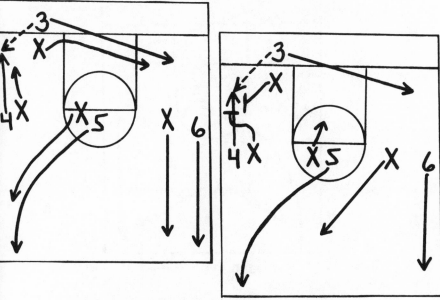

Diag. 221 Matching Up In The 1–3–2 Full-Court Press

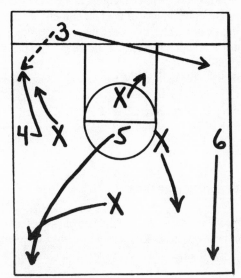

Diag. 223 Matching Up In The 1–2–1–2 Full-Court Press

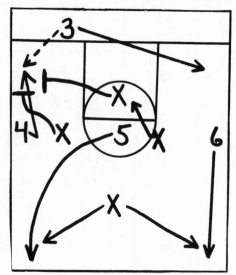

Diag. 224   Trapping In The 1–2–1–2 Full-Court Press

inbounds pass or to match up. (Diagrams 223–224) Its most widespread usage comes in trapping in any of the four corners of the half-court after the ball is inbounded. The offside wing covers return passes to the inbounder in the offside corner, and the deep ''1'' player covers both midcourt corners as before.

If the receiver is able to relay the ball quickly to a midcourt corner, the trapping movement consists of the ballside wing guard and midcourt guard advancing on the receiver. The offside wing, then, covers passes to the center of the midcourt area and the inside guard covers passes to cutters, as shown below in Diagram 225.

HALF-COURT ZONE PRESSES

Of all of the areas of concern within women's basketball, possibly no one aspect has been less heralded, or more potently adaptable as a weapon of attack, than that of the half-court presses. Due, perhaps, to the lessened

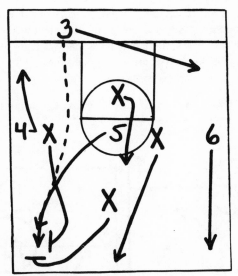

Diag. 225 Trapping In The Midcourt Corner, 1–2–1–2 Full-Court Press

chances of forcing ten-second violations, half-court presses have been largely overlooked in favor of full-court presses. Still, while it is true that the ten-second violations will likely be decreased because the offense is closer to half-court when defensive pressure is applied, there are more guards (as many as five, depending upon the press) in a smaller area of the court, thereby increasing the likelihood of stealing the ball or forcing ballhandling mistakes.

The only real problem with half-court presses is avoiding situations in which there are five guards on one side of the half-court line, although the problem is lessened by the forwards' having to avoid the same pitfall.

The 2–3–1 And 3–2–1 Half-Court Presses

Although theoretically viable, there is little occasion for using an even front defense. In fact, the only even-front half-court zone defense encountered in normal situations is the 2–3–1 half-court press. With the exception of the 2–3–1, even-fronted zones tend to negate much of the press's trapping value at the sidelines.

The 2–3–1 is an exceedingly powerful half-court pressing defense when the opponents are incapable of completing the long pass downcourt. In such cases, there may be as many as eight players within six to eight feet of the half-court line at one time.

Diag. 226 The 2–3–1 Half-Court Press, Corner Trapping

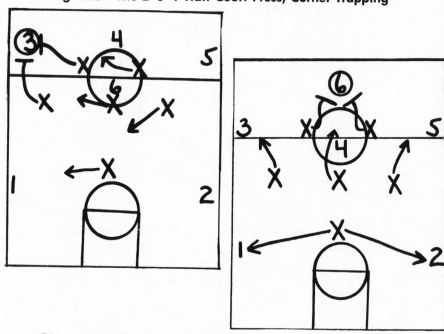

Diag. 227 The 2–3–1 Half-Court Press, Trapping In The Middle

Many teams are reluctant to attack half-court presses by matching up, preferring to split the outside guards, force the double team, then pass to an open forward at the sideline. (Diagram 228) The splitting can be dealt with easily enough by matching up defensively before trapping, since a matchup zone cannot be split offensively.

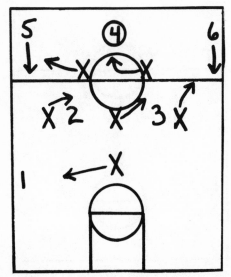

Diag. 228 Splitting The 2–3–1 Half-Court Press, With Defensive Adjustments

While weak ballhandlers can be trapped any time from a half-court alignment, strong ballhandlers should first be matched up and then steered into trapping situations. Whenever trapping occurs, it always leaves at least one guard with dual defensive responsibilities, and the defense must concentrate on stopping the ballhandler from making the pass, and ensuring that the two–on–one offensive advantage involves the two most difficult passes available to the ballhandler.

For example, assume that Team A splits the middle of the 2–3–1 half-court press, as shown in Diagram 229. If the trap is unsuccessful, either the pass to a wing (O5 or O6), or to (O2 or O3), will be clear.

The trapping movement should begin when the dribbler passes the top of the circle, in order to avoid the various situations shown in Diagram 229.

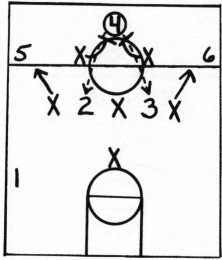

Diag. 229   Passing Routes Against Premature Trapping

The 3–2–1 is potentially as strong as any half-court press. It is essentially the same as the 2–3–1, except that the possibility of having five guards inadvertently move onto one half-court is lessened, and the 3–2–1 traps more naturally than the 2–3–1. (Diagram 232)

In the 3–2–1 alignment shown in Diagram 230, X1 and X2 are the stationary forwards, X3 and X4 are the rovers, and X5 and X6 are the stationary guards. X1 and X2 are on the defensive left side of the court because the ball usually comes up that side and they will thus be less likely to rove after they stop the dribbler. X5 plays the defensive right side because she will sometimes be required to drop back quickly to stop the opponents when they break the press. Her retreat then will be facilitated by her playing opposite the ball.

Matching up in the 3–2–1 is a simple task, with stationary forward X2 covering the dribbler as the offside wing, X3 in Diagram 238, covers cutters through the middle.

The 3–2–1 provides excellent coverage as a trapping zone. The two guards nearest the dribbler spring the trap—usually X1 and X2, as shown

Diag. 230   The 3-2-1 Half-Court Pressing Alignment

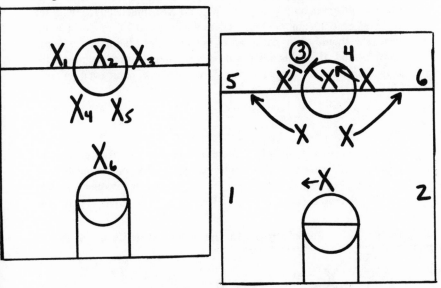

Diag. 231   Matching Up In The 3-2-1 Half-Court Press

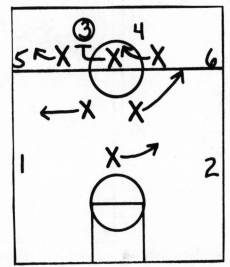

Diag. 232   Trapping In The 3-2-1 Half-Court Press

in Diagram 232. As the trapping guards move into position, the other guards match up (except deep guard X6), practically forcing the ballhandler to attempt the long pass to O1 or O2. If X6 cannot steal the pass, she should try to bat it out of bounds. When the trap is properly administered, the ballhandler will be stopped and forced to protect the ball, with only the long, lob pass down or across court even partially clear.

The 1–3–2 and 3–1–2 Half-Court Presses.

These presses are slightly more conservative in nature than the previous two because their strength apparently lies in combatting the long pass. They can be used in trapping, but they also adapt extremely well as matchup defenses. (Diagrams 233-234). The perceptive reader may have

Diag. 233 Matching Up In The 1–3–2 Half-Court Press

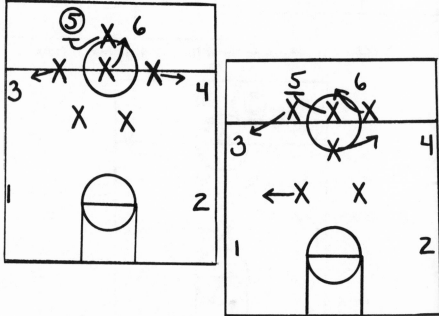

Diag. 234 Matching Up In The 3–1–2 Half-Court Press

noticed the *apparent* strength of the 1–3–2 and 3–1–2 mentioned above. Their strength lies in the fact that the ballhandler will *think* that the long passes are both covered, whereas, in reality, these presses will rotate into single deep coverage after the ballhandler receives enough defensive pressure to begin protecting the ball. Thus, she may or may not have the long pass open, depending upon the deep guard's mobility. She will be unlikely to see them, however, because of the defensive pressure exerted upon her in trapping or matching up. (Diagrams 235–236)

Diag. 235   Trapping In The 1–3–2 Half-Court Press

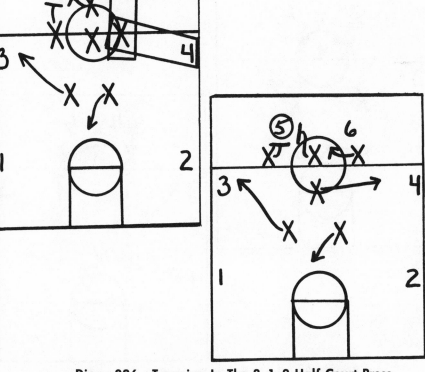

Diag. 236   Trapping In The 3–1–2 Half-Court Press

The 1–2–1–2 and 1–2–2–1 Half-Court Presses.

These presses, while virtually identical with other presses in their system of matching up, are slightly less effective in trapping. This is because the one-player offensive advantage caused by double-teaming the ballhandler occurs in the midcourt area rather than the downcourt corners. If the guards are grossly inexperienced, the defense is likely to be weak at the sidelines (1–2–1–2), or middle (1–2–2–1), but experienced or aggressive players should be able to maintain defensive control even when the trapping is unsuccessful. The following final diagrams show the matching and trapping situations.

Diag. 237   Matching Up In The 1–2–2–1 Half-Court Press

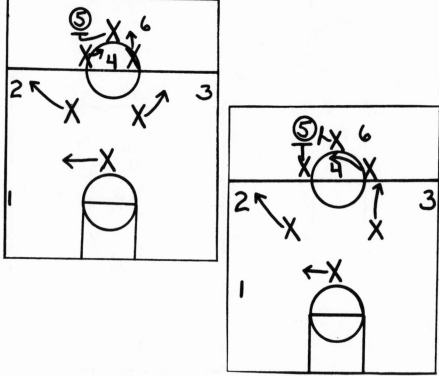

Diag. 238   Trapping In The 1–2–2–1 Half-Court Press

Diag. 239 Matching Up In The 1–2–1–2 Half-Court Press

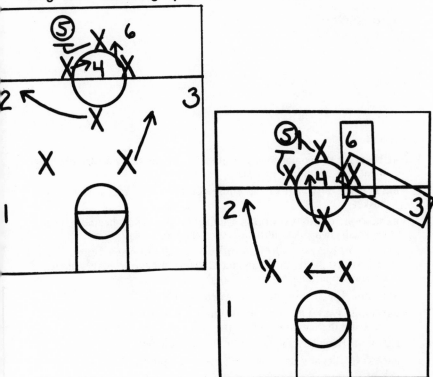

Diag. 240 Trapping In The 1–2–1–2 Half-Court Press

Glossary

AUTOMATIC A spontaneous movement to counteract defensive adjustment to a continuity offense

BACKCOURT That half of the entire court farthest from a team's own basket

BACKDOOR, GOING BACKDOOR Cutting to the basket behind a guard, especially when she turns to watch the ball

BALANCED ATTACK Offense in which all forwards either score approximately the same amount of points or have an equal number of scoring opportunities

BALLSIDE The side of the court where the ball is

BASEBALL PASS One-hand pass thrown baseball-style, as in passes covering the length of the court

BASELINE Boundary line at either end of the court

BLOCKING Illegally impeding an opponent's progress

BLOCKING OUT Positioning oneself between one's opponent and the basket after a shot has been taken

BOUNCE PASS Pass striking the floor before reaching the receiver

BREAK Move quickly from one position to another, especially from a standing start (e.g., "breaking" into the lane). Also called *cut*

BRUSH, BRUSHING OFF The act of cutting directly by a teammate with the intention of blocking a guard out of the play, as in scissoring movements.

CHEST PASS Most widely used pass in basketball, a two-hand pass pushed from the passer's chest toward the receiver so that she receives the ball in the same general area

CLEAR, CLEAROUT An isolation technique in which three forwards without the ball are on one side of the court while the fourth sets up a play or attempts to score

COMBINATION ZONE Zone defense employing both zone and player-to-player principles simultaneously. In girls' basketball, it is also called a *Triangle-One* zone defense

CONTINGENCY CUTTER Secondary receiver acting as a *safety value*, especially in the backcourt against full-court presses

CONTINUITY OFFENSE A sequence of set plays allowing repetition of an offensive pattern without the forwards' having to set up again in their basic positions

CONTROLLED OFFENSE An offensive strategy featuring ball control and preferential shot selection, although the selection is not as limited as in delays, stalls, or freezes

CONTROLLING THE BOARDS Gaining a majority of the rebounds

CORNER Area along the baseline toward either corner of that end of the court

CORNER SHOOTER Forward who specializes in shooting from the baseline

COURT BALANCE Having an equal number of forwards on both sides of the offensive court when a play begins

CUT, CUTTER Offensive move toward the basket or other specific area of the court; one who makes such a move

DEEP Near the basket

DEFENSE The team not in possession of the ball

DELAY Type of offensive strategy in which a team is content to run the clock until a specific shot (usually, a layup) can be taken

DOUBLE POST Offensive alignment with two post players

DOUBLE SCREEN Two forwards forming a single screen for a third forward

DOUBLE-TEAMING Two defenders guarding a single forward simultaneously

DOWNCOURT Toward the opposite end of the court

DRIVE A dribbling movement toward the basket

DRIVING THE BASELINE Driving around a defender by dribbling toward the baseline rather than the center of the court

FAKE Any individual movement with or without the ball designed to deceive one's guard

FAST BREAK An attempt by the offense to move the ball downcourt quickly in order to shoot before the defense is organized

FIGURE-EIGHT Weave pattern involving three forwards, whose movements follow the path of an imaginary figure eight on the court

FILLING THE LANES In a fast break, moving into assigned dribbling or passing areas

FORECOURT The area between midcourt and the offensive team's baseline

FORWARD Any offensive player

FREE-LANCING Spontaneous, unpatterned offensive movements

FREE THROW An unguarded shot from the free throw line, the successful completion of which gives that team one point. Free throws are awarded as a result of personal or technical fouls. Also called foul shot

FREEZING A GUARD, FREEZING THE DEFENSE Any offensive movement, especially dribbling, that stops the movement of one or more guards, or denies them the opportunity to switch defensive responsibilities—in effect, momentarily "freezing" them in one position on the floor

FREEZING THE BALL Offensive strategy in which the forwards attempt to retain ball possession for prolonged periods of time without attempting to score. Sometimes called a *stall*, freezing usually occurs late in games to protect a lead

FRONTING Defensive technique in which a guard assumes a defensive position between her forward and the ball

GIVE-AND-GO Fundamental offensive pattern consisting of a pass and cut away from the ball

GUARD Any defensive player

HALF-COURT LINE The line dividing a basketball court into two equal halves

HIGH-LOW POST See *Tandem Post*

HIGH-PERCENTAGE SHOT Any shot, taken from any area of the court, that a player is capable of making on most attempts

HIGH POST Stationary offensive position in the vicinity of the free throw line

HOOK SHOT A one-handed shot accomplished by shooting the ball from the *side* of one's body in a circular movement

I-FORMATION Bringin alignment with three forwards lining up perpendicular to the boundary line in single file

INSIDE In or toward the free throw lane

INSIDE GUARDS Guards nearest to the basket

JUMP SHOT A one-handed shot accomplished by shooting the ball while in the air after jumping

KEY Any movement of signal that initiates an offensive sequence. Also, the vicinity of the free throw line

LANE The free throw lane

LAYUP Shot taken near the basket after a dribble or cut to the basket

LEAD PASS Pass thrown to an intended area in front of or beyond a moving player

LOW POST Stationary position near the baseline adjacent to the free throw lane

MAN-TO-MAN DEFENSE See *Player-To-Player Defense*

MATCHUP, MATCHING UP Defensive movement resulting in one-on-one coverage

MIDCOURT The area between the half-court line and a line extending across the court twenty-eight feet from the offensive baseline. Two lines at the sidelines mark the beginnings of this imaginary crosscourt line

MIDDLE Toward the center of the free throw lane, (e.g., driving "down the middle.")

OFFENSE The team in possession of the ball

OFFSIDE The side of the court away from the ball

ONE-ON-ONE Situation in which one forward attempts to score against one guard

OUTLET PASS Any pass that begins an offensive movement or pattern, especially passing to a teammate breaking downcourt after a defensive rebound

OUTSIDE GUARDS Defenders farthest from the basket

OVERGUARDING A defensive stance in which a forward is guarded by exaggeratedly overplaying her toward whichever side of her the ball is on

OVERLOAD Attacking a zone defense by placing three, and possibly four, forwards on the same side of the court

PASSING LANE Route to the basket taken by the forwards without the ball in a fast break situation

PENETRATION The act of passing or dribbling the ball into the area near the basket

PICK A legal moving screen occurring naturally as part of a sequence of offensive movements. For simplicity, the term *screen* has been used in this book to denote both screens and picks

PIVOTING Turning on one foot

PLAYER-TO-PLAYER DEFENSE Team defense characterized by each defender's guarding an assigned player, regardless of her position on the court

POINT, POINT FORWARD Offensive position at the top of the circle; one who plays the point. Also, the forward leading a fast break

POST Stationary offensive position near the basket, designated *high post* or *low post*. Also called pivot

PRESS Defensive situation in which the offense receives defensive pressure throughout the length of the court, three-quarters of the court, or half of the court

PRESSING, OR PRESSURE, DEFENSE Defensive strategy in which the forwards receive constant defensive pressure at their end of the court

PRIMARY RECEIVER Among several possible pass receivers, the preferred target

REBOUND Recovery from the backboard of a missed field goal or free throw attempt

REVERSE PIVOT Backward turning movement

ROLL Pivoting move toward the basket or in front of a guard

ROTATION Movement of players or the ball from one side of the court to the other

ROVERS Girls permitted by the rules to cross the half-court line to play at either end of the court. Each team is allowed two rovers

RUNNING THE CLOCK Holding the ball without attempting to score while the game clock is running

SAFETY FORWARD Forward who drops back to the vicinity of half-court to stop potential fast breaks

SAFETY VALVE A forward whose cut occurs only after the other forwards' cuts have been unsuccessful

SCISSORING Crossing movement by two or more outside forwards, sometimes preliminary to splitting the post

SCREEN A movement to legally position oneself in front of, behind, or to the side of a guard in such a manner that a teammate will be free to drive or shoot. Also called *pick*

SCREEN-AND-ROLL Offensive maneuver in which the person setting the screen pivots and cuts toward the basket when the guards switch

SEAM The overlapping area of responsibility between any two guards in a zone defense

SECONDARY RECEIVER Any potential pass receiver other than the primary receiver

SET PLAY An orderly, prearranged sequence of offensive moves designed to yield scoring opportunities

SET SHOT Shot taken with one or both feet remaining on the floor

SET UP Assume, or return to, one's basic position on either offense or defense

SHUFFLE Continuity offense featuring a great deal of movement away from the ball

SIDELINE Boundary line on either side of the court

SINKING Defensive technique involving dropping off one's forward to aid in defending against the opponent's inside game. Also called *sagging*

SLOWDOWN Offensive tactic related to stalls, in which the emphasis is on ball control and shot selectivity. Generally, slowdowns are used to "slow down" a faster opponent, rather than to merely run down the clock

SPLITTING A ZONE Setting up offensively in such a manner that the guards are unable to match up defensively with the forwards

SPLITTING THE POST Offensive technique involving two or more outside forwards cutting around a stationary forward

STALL Offensive tactic emphasizing ball retention rather than attempting to score. Should not be confused with controlled offenses, slowdowns, or delays, since stalls are often of gamewide duration

STATIONARY FORWARD, STATIONARY GUARD Player who remains at one end of the court when the ball is at the other end

SWITCHING Defense maneuver involving two or more guards trading defensive responsibilities, usually in response to offensive maneuvers such as *screening* or *scissoring*

TANDEM POST Double post consisting of high and low-post players. Also called *high-low post*

TEN-SECOND LINE The half-court line, beyond which the offensive team must advance the ball within ten seconds after gaining possession of the ball in the defensive court

THREE-ON-TWO Offensive situation in which three forwards attempt to score against two guards, usually occurring at the end of a fast break

THREE-SECOND LANE The offensive free throw lane. Forwards are not allowed to remain inside the lane for more than three consecutive seconds

TIPPING, WINNING/LOSING THE TIP Shooting or passing the ball by tapping it with extended fingers, as in rebounded shots or jump ball situations

TOP, TOP OF THE CIRCLE That part of the free throw circle nearest to midcourt

TRAILER Offensive player behind (trailing), the dribbler, especially in fast breaking situations

TRAILING WING In a fast break, the forward behind, and to the side of, the point forward

TRAPPING Defensive maneuver involving two or more guards covering one forward simultaneously in order to steal the ball or otherwise gain a defensive advantage. Also called double or triple-teaming

TRIANGLE-ONE Defense involving three guards playing a zone defense while the fourth covers her forward player-to-player

TURNOVER Offensive mistake resulting in loss of ball possession without a shot having been taken. Also, rotating the offense from one side of the court to the other, as in "turning the ball over to the other side of the court"

TYING UP THE BALL Bringing about a jump ball situation

WEAVE Continuity offense involving repetition of an outside crossing pattern by the forwards

WHEEL Continuity offense featuring cuts and reverses off inside screens

WING, OR WING FORWARD Player whose original offensive position is outside on either side of the court

ZONE DEFENSE Team defense in which the guards are assigned coverage of specific areas of the court rather than specific players

Bibliography

Cousy, Bob, and Power, Frank. *Basketball Concepts And Techniques*. Boston: Allyn & Bacon, Inc., 1970.

Gardner, Jack. *Championship Basketball*. Englewood Cliffs, N.J.: Prentice-Hall, 1961.

Jucker, Ed. *Cincinnati Power Basketball*. Englewood Cliffs, N.J.: Prentice-Hall, 1962.

Meyer, Margaret, and Schwartz, Marguerite. *Team Sports For Girls and Women*. Philadelphia: W.B. Saunders Co., 1957.

Miller, Donna Mae, and Ley, Katherine L. *Individual And Team Sports For Women*. Englewood Cliffs, N.J.: Prentice-Hall, 1955.

Neal, Patsy. *Basketball Techniques For Women*. New York: Ronald Press, 1966.

Schaafsma, Frances. *Women's Basketball*. Dubuque, Iowa: William C. Brown Co., 1966.

Sports Illustrated, ed. *Sports Illustrated Book Of Basketball*. Philadelphia and New York: J.B. Lippincott Co., 1962.

Stutts, Ann. *Women's Basketball*. Pacific Palisades, Calif.: Goodyear Publishing Co., 1969.

Vannier, Maryhelen, and Poindexter, Hally Beth. *Individual And Team Sports For Girls And Women*. Philadelphia: W.B. Saunders Co., 1960.

Wooden, John. *Practical Modern Basketball*. New York: Ronald Press, 1966.

———. *1973-74 Basketball Rule Book*. Elgin, Illinois: National Federation Of State High School Associations, 1974.

Index